KALLIS' iBT TOEFL® PATTERN

Listening 1

TOEFL® is a registered trademark of Educational Testing Services (ETS), Princeton, New Jersey, USA. The content in this text, including the practice questions, Hacking Strategy, and Quick Look, is created and designed exclusively by KALLIS. This publication is not endorsed or approved by ETS.

KALLIS' iBT TOEFL® Pattern Listening 1

KALLIS EDU, INC.
7490 Opportunity Road, Suite 203
San Diego, CA 92111
(858) 277-8600
info@kallisedu.com
www.kallisedu.com

Copyright © 2015 KALLIS EDU, INC.

All rights reserved. No part of this book may be reproduced, stored in a retrieval system, or transmitted in any form or by any means, electronic or mechanical, including photocopying, recording, or otherwise, without the prior written permission of the copyright owner.

ISBN-10: 1-5077-4271-1
ISBN-13: 978-1-5077-4271-6

iBT TOEFL® Pattern - Listening I is the first of our three-level iBT TOEFL® Listening Exam preparation book series.

Our **iBT TOEFL® Pattern Listening** series simplifies each TOEFL Listening question type into a series of simple steps, which ensures that students do not become overwhelmed as they develop their listening skills. Moreover, our commitment to minimizing instruction and maximizing student practice assures that students have many opportunities to strengthen their listening skills.

KALLIS

KALLIS'

TOEFL® iBT PATTERN LISTENING 1

CONCENTRATE

Getting Started

A study guide should familiarize the reader with the material found on the test, develop methods that can be used to solve various question types, and provide plenty of practice questions. KALLIS' iBT TOEFL® Pattern Series aims to accomplish all these tasks by presenting iBT TOEFL® test material in an organized, comprehensive, and easy-to-understand way.

KALLIS' iBT TOEFL® Pattern Listening Series shows students how to identify and solve each question type found on the iBT TOEFL Listening section. Thus, students can identify which types of questions they find most challenging, and then develop strategies for solving them. Additionally, each book in our Pattern Listening Series contains hundreds of practice questions, ensuring that students can develop the skills they need to succeed on the iBT TOEFL.

Putting the Questions into Context

Chapters 1 and 2

- These chapters provide general information about what you will listen to during the iBT TOEFL Listening section.
- These chapters explain and provide focused practice for each type of multiple-choice question found on the iBT TOEFL Listening section.
- Each listening passage in these chapters includes **Key Terms, Vocabulary,** and **Notes** sections to help you organize your thoughts as you listen.
- These chapters conclude with **Exercises** allow you to practice the skills in a longer format.

Enhancing Test-Taking Skills through Practice

Chapters 3 and 4

▶ Located in Chapter 3, **Actual Practices** provide listening passages (conversations and lectures) with multiple question types. In order to complete these, you must combine skills that you developed in Chapters 1 and 2.

▶ Located in Chapter 4, the **Actual Test** is meant to familiarize you with the format of the official iBT TOEFL Listening test. Thus, you should be familiar with all question types before attempting to complete the **Actual Test**.

▶ A scaled scoring chart is located at the beginning of the **Actual Test**, so you can grade yourself and get an idea of how you might score on the official iBT TOEFL Listening section.

Checking Your Own Progress

Chapters 5 and 6

▶ The **Appendix** in Chapter 5 contains transcripts of all the conversations and lectures found throughout this book.

▶ The **Answer Key** in Chapter 6 contains the correct answers to all multiple-choice questions found throughout this book. It also includes answer explanations and example notes that can help guide your studies.

▶ If you do not want to repeatedly flip to the back of the book for answers, simply cut out the **Simple Answers** at the very back of the book. **Simple Answers** provides a quick reference so you can confirm that all your answers are correct.

Table of Contents

Chapter 1

Campus-Related Conversations — 1
Type 1: Main Idea — 4
    Main Idea Questions — 6
Type 2: Detail — 10
    Detail Questions — 12
Type 3: Purpose — 16
    Purpose Questions — 18
Type 4: Inference — 22
    Inference Questions — 24

Exercise 1 — 28
Exercise 2 — 30
Exercise 3 — 32
Exercise 4 — 34
Exercise 5 — 36

Chapter 2

Academic Lectures — 39
Type 1: Main Idea — 42
    Main Idea Questions — 44
Type 2: Detail — 48
    Detail Questions — 50
Type 3: Purpose — 54
    Purpose Questions — 56
Type 4: Inference — 60
    Inference Questions — 62

Exercise 1 — 66
Exercise 2 — 68
Exercise 3 — 70
Exercise 4 — 72
Exercise 5 — 74

LISTENING 1 CONCENTRATE

Chapter 3

Actual Practices 77
Actual Practice 1 78
Actual Practice 2 84
Actual Practice 3 90
Actual Practice 4 96
Actual Practice 5 102
Actual Practice 6 108

Chapter 4

Actual Test 115
Listening Passage 1 116
Listening Passage 2 118
Listening Passage 3 120
Listening Passage 4 122
Listening Passage 5 124
Listening Passage 6 126

Appendix

Listening Scripts 129
Chapter 1   130
Chapter 2   137
Chapter 3   143
Chapter 4   151

Appendix

Answer Key 155
Chapter 1   156
Chapter 2   160
Chapter 3   166
Chapter 4   174

Appendix

Simple Answers 179

Before You Begin...

OVERVIEW

The iBT TOEFL Listening section consists of four to six academic lectures and two to three campus-related conversations. At the end of each lecture, you must answer six multiple-choice questions, and at the end of each conversation, you must answer five multiple-choice questions. The Listening section takes 60 to 90 minutes to complete. Each lecture and conversation is 3 to 6 minutes long.

> **Note** Because this is the introductory book in the series, the conversations and lectures in this book are shorter and use simpler language than those you will encounter on the iBT TOEFL.

LISTENING CONTENT

The lecture portions of the Listening section will consist of a professor discussing a topic that you might hear in an introductory-level university course. Because these Listening-section lectures replicate lectures that you might hear at an American university, you should expect the professor to pause, stammer, digress, and repeat himself or herself.

The conversation portions of the Listening section will consist of a dialogue between a student and a professor or some other university employee. If students are speaking to a professor, they will discuss something related to the professor's class, such as a student's project, the contents of a recent lecture, or classroom rules. If students are talking to any other university employee, they will discuss something related to campus life, such as class registration, housing concerns, or financial aid. The speakers in the conversations will use normal speech patterns, including pauses, stammers, and repetition.

LISTENING SECTION QUESTIONS

Once you have finished listening to a lecture/conversation, you will be asked to answer several multiple-choice questions. Some questions will ask you to select one correct answer, some will ask you to select more than one correct answer, and others will ask you to fill out a small table or chart. Each question will fall under one of four broad categories: Main Idea Questions, Detail Questions, Purpose Questions, or Inference Questions.

TAKING NOTES

Because you will only hear each lecture and conversation once, taking notes is important. But knowing what to include in your notes can be difficult: trying to write down everything you hear will reduce your comprehension of the lecture or conversation, yet taking few notes might make answering the multiple choice questions difficult or impossible.

Therefore, write down information from the lecture or conversation if it addresses one of the following three questions:

1) *What* is the lecture mainly about?
2) *Why* is the speaker discussing this topic?
3) *How* is the speaker structuring the information?

Addressing question (1) in your notes will help you identify the lecture or conversation's main idea and details; addressing question (2) will help you identify the purpose of the lecture or conversation; and addressing question (3) will help you understand the passage fully.

SYMBOLS AND ABBREVIATIONS

When taking notes, save time by using **symbols** instead of words. In addition to using the symbols in the chart that follows, you can create your own symbols.

Symbol	Meaning	Symbol	Meaning
&	and	=	equals, is
%	percent	>	more than
#	number	<	less than
@	at	→	resulting in
↓	decreasing	↑	increasing

ABBREVIATIONS FOR UNIVERSITY ACTIVITIES

Abbreviation	Meaning	Abbreviation	Meaning
edu.	education	RA	resident assistant
GE	general education	stu.	student
GPA	grade point average	TA	teaching assistant
prof.	professor/professional	univ.	university

ABBREVIATIONS FOR ACADEMIC TOPICS

Abbreviation	Meaning	Abbreviation	Meaning
bio.	biology/biological	exp.	experience/experiment
c.	century	info.	information
chem.	chemistry/chemical	gov.	government
def.	definition	hyp.	hypothesis
dic.	dictionary	psych.	psychology
econ.	economics/economy	theo.	theory
env.	environment	vocab.	vocabulary

OTHER ABBREVIATIONS

Abbreviation	Meaning	Abbreviation	Meaning
abt.	about	min.	minute
b/c	because	pic.	picture
comm.	community/communication	ppl.	people
ex.	example	pref.	preference
fam.	family	pt.	point
fav.	favorite	ques.	question
gen.	general/generation	s/b	somebody
H2O	water	s/o	someone
hr.	hour	sec.	second
impt.	important	w/i	within
loc.	location	w/o	without
lvl.	level	yr.	year

CHAPTER 1

Campus-Related Conversations

Chapter 1

Campus-Related Conversations

EXPLANATION OF TASK

Each iBT TOEFL Listening section will include two or three campus-related conversations. The speakers in these conversations will discuss issues that you may encounter as a student at an American university. The conversations are generally between a university student and a university employee. Some common conversation topics include:

- students asking their professors about project or research-paper requirements
- students asking their professors for clarification regarding confusing class materials
- students asking university employees for advice on academic, financial, or housing matters
- students discussing a campus issue or a class assignment with each other

Each conversation is 3 to 5 minutes long. Because these conversations are supposed to replicate natural-sounding speech in an American university setting, the speakers may use English speech patterns such as repetition, digression from the main topic, false starts, pauses, and fillers (um, uh, eh, well). You will hear each conversation only once, so you are encouraged to take notes as you listen.

After you have listened to the conversation, you must answer five multiple-choice questions that relate to the contents of the conversation. These questions will be related to the main idea, purpose, organization, or implications of the conversation. You may use any notes that you have written down when answering the multiple-choice questions.

 Because this is the introductory-level book in the series, the conversations in this book are shorter and use simpler language than those you will encounter on the iBT TOEFL.

NECESSARY SKILLS

In order to successfully complete the conversation portions of the Listening section, you must be able to:

- comprehend vocabulary regarding a variety of campus-related issues
- take notes on conversational English
- summarize spoken information
- recognize the main idea and details of a spoken conversation
- determine the purpose of a spoken conversation
- make inferences about the organization and content of a spoken conversation
- make inferences about the tones and attitudes of the speakers

Question Types

The iBT TOEFL Listening section consists of four main types of questions.

1 Main Idea Questions

Main Idea Questions require you to identify the main topic of the conversation. Because the answers to these questions are drawn directly from the conversation content, taking notes may prove helpful when answering these questions.

2 Detail Questions

Detail Questions require you to identify a detail, an example, or an explanation related to the main idea of the conversation. Because the answers to these questions are drawn directly from the conversation content, taking notes may prove helpful when answering these questions.

3 Purpose Questions

Purpose Questions require you to identify *why* a speaker makes a particular statement or asks a particular question Therefore, when listening to the conversation, concentrate on fully comprehending the purpose of the conversation.

4 Inference Questions

Inference Questions require you to make an *inference*, or assumption, based on the contents of the conversation. An inference question might ask you to identify the speaker's tone or the conversation's basic structure.

Conversation Question Type 1: Main Idea

WHAT IS A MAIN IDEA QUESTION?

The *main idea*, or topic, is the overall subject of the conversation. Be careful when answering a **Main Idea Question**: the speakers will not always directly state their main ideas. Therefore, you may have to infer the main idea based on the context of the conversation. Some conversations will not contain any **Main Idea Questions** while others will ask one **Main Idea Question**. If it appears, the **Main Idea Question** will be the first question you are asked.

HOW TO TAKE NOTES

When taking notes on a campus-related conversation, the main idea will likely be one of the first things that you write down. As you listen to the conversation, ask yourself, "**WHAT** is the conversation about?" Asking this question will make identifying and answering the **Main Idea Question** easier.

MAIN IDEA QUESTION FORMATS

Main Idea Questions usually ask you to identify the main idea, issue, or topic presented in the conversation. Common formats for **Main Idea Questions** include:

> *What is the conversation mainly about?*
> *Why does the student visit the professor/advisor/university employee?*
> *What is the main issue being discussed in the conversation?*

 Main Idea Questions that begin with "why" are very similar in structure to **Purpose Questions** (page 16). But **Main Idea Questions** that begin with "why" ask for the main purpose of the conversation, while **Purpose Questions** ask *why* the speaker discusses certain details and examples.

TIPS

Listening Tips: When listening for **Main Idea Questions**, focus on information presented at the beginning of the conversation. This part of the conversation sometimes contains important words, phrases, and sentences that indicate the main idea.

Answer Tips: In questions about the topic, main idea, or main purpose, the correct answer will deal with the overall subject of the conversation. Incorrect answer choices will be:

- broader than the focus of the conversation
- details of the conversation, not the main idea
- inaccurate or untrue according to the speaker
- about a subject not mentioned in the conversation

Main Idea Questions

Listen to **Track 1.01**. Take notes using the template below as you listen to the conversation.

Key Terms
- research paper
- rewrite
- evidence

Vocabulary
- "refresh my memory" (idiom): remind me
- sufficient (adj): enough, satisfactory

Things to Consider

WHAT is the conversation about?

Notes

stu. → asks prof. for advice, wants to rewrite research ppr.

prof. → says stu. needs to support ideas w/ evidence

_____

Answer the following multiple-choice question.

Why does the student visit his professor?
(A) To ask for a better grade on his paper
(B) To get help with rewriting his paper
(C) To learn about democracy in ancient Athens
(D) To review a concept presented in class

Answer Explanation

Toward the beginning of the conversation, the student asks the professor for "some advice for rewriting" his paper. Because the rest of the conversation is about the student's paper and the professor's advice for rewriting it, the correct answer must be **Choice B**.

Main Idea Questions

Listen to **Track 1.02**. Take notes using the template below as you listen to the conversation.

Key Terms
- on-campus jobs
- dining hall positions
- application

Vocabulary
- freshman (n): a first-year high school or university student

Things to Consider

WHAT is the conversation about?

Notes
_____
_____
_____

Answer the following multiple-choice question.

1) What are the student and the university employee mainly discussing?
   (A) Where to find the employment office
   (B) Meal options at the dining hall
   (C) On-campus job opportunities
   (D) How to apply for financial aid

Main Idea Questions

Listen to **Track 1.03**. Take notes using the template below as you listen to the conversation.

Key Terms

harmonica
Richter

Vocabulary

range (n): an area of uninhabited land, usually used for hunting or grazing

Things to Consider

WHAT is the conversation about?

Notes

_____
_____
_____

Answer the following multiple-choice question.

2) What is the conversation mainly about?
   (A) How the harmonica influenced America
   (B) European and American harmonicas
   (C) Famous harmonica players
   (D) The origins of the harmonica

Main Idea Questions

Listen to **Track 1.04**. Take notes using the template below as you listen to the conversation.

Key Terms
advanced genetics class
organic chemistry

Vocabulary
lower-division classes: university courses that one must take before taking major-specific courses
upper-division classes: university courses related to a specific major or area of study

Things to Consider

WHAT is the conversation about?

Notes
_____
_____
_____

Answer the following multiple-choice question.

3) Why does the student visit the professor?
   (A) To ask if she should take a particular science class
   (B) To complain about the difficulty of the professor's class
   (C) To learn what grade she has in the professor's class
   (D) To tell the professor that she plans to drop his class

Main Idea Questions

Listen to **Track 1.05**. Take notes using the template below as you listen to the conversation.

Key Terms
- resident assistant
- academic records
- application
- interview

Vocabulary
- resident assistant (n): a student who is trained to supervise students living in on-campus dorms or apartments

Things to Consider

WHAT is the conversation about?

Notes
_____
_____
_____

Answer the following multiple-choice question.

4) What is the conversation mainly about?
   (A) Applying for a resident assistant position
   (B) Requesting an official university transcript
   (C) Quitting an on-campus job
   (D) Complaining about a bad resident assistant

Conversation Question Type 2: Detail

WHAT IS A DETAIL QUESTION?

Details are specific pieces of information that relate to a larger topic. These pieces of information can be facts, descriptions, reasons, examples, or opinions. **Detail Questions** will ask you to recall specific information from the conversation. There will be one to three **Detail Questions** in each campus-related conversation.

HOW TO TAKE NOTES

When taking notes on a campus-related conversation, you will notice that the details are distributed throughout the conversation. Focus on writing down only details that relate to the main idea of the conversation. **Before taking notes, try to identify the main topic of the conversation.**

As you listen to the conversation, ask yourself, "**WHAT** details contribute to the main idea?" Answering this question will make identifying and answering the **Detail Questions** easier.

DETAIL QUESTION FORMATS

Detail Questions will ask you to identify specific details, explanations, examples, or opinions that relate to the main topic of the conversation. Common formats for **Detail Questions** include:

> *What does the speaker say about _____ in the conversation?*
> *According to the speaker, what/why/where/when/how _____?*
> *What is the speaker's opinion of _____?*

Whereas **Main Idea Questions** always appear as multiple-choice questions with one correct answer, **Detail Questions** will have one, two, or three correct answers.

TIPS

Listening Tips: When listening, notice information that contributes to the main idea of the conversation. This information may involve information such as numbers, dates, names, definitions, reasons, connections, choices, and processes.

Answer Tips: In questions about details, the correct answer will always restate facts, descriptions, reasons, examples, or opinions from the lecture. When you answer **Detail Questions**, try to recall exactly what was said by the speaker. Look at your notes if you cannot remember exactly what was said. Incorrect answer choices may:

- repeat some of the speaker's words but convey a different meaning
- use words that sound like, but are actually different from, the speaker's words
- be inaccurate or irrelevant based on what you hear in the conversation

Detail Questions

Listen to **Track 1.06**. Take notes using the template below as you listen to the conversation.

Key Terms

dances
"shocking"
"traditional"

Vocabulary

conservative (adj): maintaining traditional values and morals
ballroom dance: a broad term that can refer to numerous types of dances performed with a partner
condemn (v): show disapproval toward

Things to Consider

WHAT is the conversation about?

WHAT details contribute to the main idea?

Notes

stu. → asks prof. abt. changes in attitude toward dances

shocking dances → traditional over time

ex: relig. program now encourages dances, used to disapprove

Answer the following multiple-choice questions.

How do people's attitudes toward new types of dance change over time?
(A) People combine different types of dance.
(B) People quickly lose interest.
(C) People become more accepting.
(D) People become more suspicious

What program inspired the student to ask the professor his question?
(A) A televised classical music concert
(B) A religious television program
(C) A television program on ballroom dance
(D) A television program on musical history

Answer Explanation

The professor confirms that "shocking" dances "often become considered 'traditional' over time." Thus, we know that people become more accepting of new dances over time, so the correct answer is **Choice C**.

Answer Explanation

When the professor asks why the student was thinking about dance and culture, the student responds that he "was watching this conservative religious program." Thus, the correct answer must be **Choice B**.

Detail Questions

Practice 1

Listen to **Track 1.07**. Take notes using the template below as you listen to the conversation.

Key Terms
noise complaint

Vocabulary
"keep it down" (idiom): be quiet

Things to Consider

WHAT is the conversation about?

WHAT details contribute to the main idea?

Notes
_____
_____
_____

Answer the following multiple-choice questions.

1) What happens when a student receives three noise complaints?
   (A) The student must go to the housing office.
   (B) The student must take extra classes.
   (C) The student cannot live in the dorms.
   (D) The student cannot listen to music.

2) How did the student find out about the noise complaint?
   (A) He received an email.
   (B) His friend delivered it to him.
   (C) He was visited by a campus security officer.
   (D) He found a notice in his campus mailbox.

Detail Questions

Practice 2

Listen to **Track 1.08**. Take notes using the template below as you listen to the conversation.

Key Terms
Romantic literature
European scientific revolution

Vocabulary
vastness (n): immensity, largeness in size

Things to Consider

WHAT is the conversation about?

WHAT details contribute to the main idea?

Notes
_____
_____
_____

Answer the following multiple-choice questions.

3) According to the student, what did the scientific revolution emphasize?
   (A) Humanity's ability to help the needy
   (B) Humanity's ability to create large machines
   (C) Humanity's understanding of nature
   (D) Humanity's need to travel the world

4) What features of nature did Romantic literature emphasize?
   Choose 2 answers.
   (A) Immensity
   (B) Loneliness
   (C) Beauty
   (D) Mystery

Detail Questions

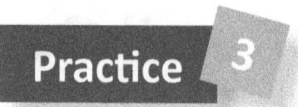

Listen to **Track 1.09**. Take notes using the template below as you listen to the conversation.

Key Terms
loan   scholarship
grant

Vocabulary
federal (adj): having to do with the United States' central government
extracurricular (adj): relating to activities pursued outside of compulsory studies; after-school activities

Things to Consider

WHAT is the conversation about?

WHAT details contribute to the main idea?

Notes
_____
_____
_____

Answer the following multiple-choice questions.

5) According to the advisor, to whom are grants given?
  (A) Students who attended community college
  (B) Students who need financial assistance
  (C) Students who did poorly in high school
  (D) Students who did not receive scholarships

6) What is one way that a loan is different from a grant?
  (A) Loans are only available once per year.
  (B) Loans are harder to get.
  (C) Loans are only available to U.S. citizens.
  (D) Loans must be paid back with interest.

Detail Questions

Listen to **Track 1.10**. Take notes using the template below as you listen to the conversation.

Key Terms
- transfer
- robotics
- Upstate University
- electrical engineering

Vocabulary
- transfer (v): to move from one place to another
- general education classes: classes or subjects that all students at a university must complete
- requirement (n): something that is necessary

Things to Consider

WHAT is the conversation about?

WHAT details contribute to the main idea?

Notes

_____
_____
_____

Answer the following multiple-choice questions.

7) Which university is the student considering transferring to?
   (A) Upstate University
   (B) Coast University
   (C) Robotics University
   (D) United University

8) What subject is the student currently studying?
   (A) Physics
   (B) General education
   (C) Electrical engineering
   (D) Robotics

CAMPUS-RELATED CONVERSATIONS ♦ CHAPTER 1

Conversation Question Type 3: Purpose

WHAT IS A PURPOSE QUESTION?

The "purpose" of a statement is the speaker's intention; you must infer purpose based on what the speaker says. In some **Purpose Questions**, you will listen to part of the conversation again before answering. There are usually one or two **Purpose Questions** that accompany each campus-related conversation.

HOW TO TAKE NOTES

The speakers usually state their purpose early in the conversation and continue to imply it through what they say and ask. **When taking notes on the purpose of the conversation, try to quickly identify the main idea.**

As you listen to the conversation, ask yourself, "**WHY** are the speakers having the conversation?" Doing so will make identifying and answering **Purpose Questions** easier.

PURPOSE QUESTION FORMATS

Purpose Questions will usually ask you why a speaker made certain claims. Common formats for **Purpose Questions** include:

> *Why does the student/professor mention _____?*
> *Why does the student/professor say this?*

 For information on questions that ask about the *main* purpose of a conversation, see page 4.

TIPS

Listening Tips: When listening for the purpose of a statement or a claim, you must rely on your ability to draw logical conclusions as to *why* the conversation is taking place or *why* a statement is being made. Your notes may help you piece together information.

Answer Tips: The correct answers to **Purpose Questions** may be implied. Thus, these questions are slightly more difficult to answer than **Main Idea** or **Detail Questions**. When answering **Purpose Questions**, look at your notes if you cannot remember exactly what the speakers said. Incorrect answer choices may:

- repeat some of the speaker's words but convey a different meaning
- be inaccurate based on what you hear in the conversation
- be irrelevant and not about anything mentioned in the conversation

Purpose Questions

Listen to **Track 1.11**. Take notes using the template below as you listen to the conversation.

Key Terms
formation of the solar system
review

Vocabulary
formation (n): development; the process of being formed
"go over" (idiom): examine, discuss

Things to Consider

WHY are the speakers having the conversation?

Notes
stu. → late for class, asks prof. for lecture info.

prof. → reviewed info. from last week

Answer the following multiple-choice questions.

Why does the student go to the professor's office hours?
(A) To complain about a confusing lecture
(B) To find out what was discussed in class
(C) To tell the professor that she likes his class
(D) To return a borrowed textbook

Listen to **Track 1.12**.
Why does the student say this?
(A) She is sorry that she missed the lecture.
(B) She is excited to learn about the solar system.
(C) She is confused by the professor's response.
(D) She is happy that she did not miss new information.

Answer Explanation
The student says that she "missed the first ten minutes of class," so she wants to know what she missed. Therefore, the correct answer must be **Choice B**.

Answer Explanation
When the student says "Oh, awesome," she is expressing happiness. We can conclude that she is happy because she did not miss any new information, even though she was late for that day's lecture. The correct answer must be **Choice D**.

Purpose Questions

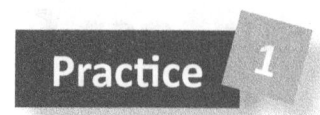

Listen to **Track 1.13**. Take notes using the template below as you listen to the conversation.

Key Terms

main campus library
engineering books
Science and Engineering library

Vocabulary

"point out" (idiom): show me
"no wonder" (idiom): it is not surprising

Things to Consider

WHY are the speakers having the conversation?

Notes

_____
_____
_____

Answer the following multiple-choice questions.

1) Why does the student approach the librarian?
   (A) To complain about a missing book
   (B) To ask for directions
   (C) To ask where the engineering books are
   (D) To find out how to volunteer at the library

2) Listen to **Track 1.14**.
   Why does the student say this?
   (A) To explain why she needs help
   (B) To explain why she is in the library
   (C) To explain why she is studying engineering
   (D) To explain why she is excited to speak with the librarian

Purpose Questions

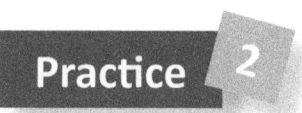

Listen to **Track 1.15**. Take notes using the template below as you listen to the conversation.

Key Terms

book recommendations
anthropology and mythology
James Frazer
The Golden Bough

Vocabulary

anthropology (n): the study of human cultures and societies
dated (adj): old-fashioned, out-of-date
ambitious (adj): describing someone or something that sets high goals

Things to Consider

WHY are the speakers having the conversation?

Notes

_____
_____
_____

Answer the following multiple-choice questions.

3) Why does the student visit the professor?
   (A) To ask about something that he said in class
   (B) To ask for book recommendations
   (C) To explain a controversial viewpoint
   (D) To ask about the life of James Frazer

4) Listen to **Track 1.16**.
   Why does the student say this?
   (A) She wants to finish the book quickly.
   (B) She does not have much time to read.
   (C) She is a very slow reader.
   (D) She does not know a lot about anthropology.

Purpose Questions

Listen to **Track 1.17**. Take notes using the template below as you listen to the conversation.

Key Terms
- library books
- policy
- late fees

Vocabulary
- overdue (adj): not there at the proper time; late
- check out (phrasal verb): (in relation to library books) borrow for a set period of time

Things to Consider

WHY are the speakers having the conversation?

Notes
_____
_____
_____

Answer the following multiple-choice questions.

5) Why does the student approach the librarian?
   (A) To pay late fees on some library books
   (B) To learn about the library's rules
   (C) To ask for a tour of the library
   (D) To return some library books

6) Listen to **Track 1.18**.
   Why does the student say this?
   (A) To explain why he turned the books in late
   (B) To convince the librarian not to make him pay late fees
   (C) To ask if he can keep the books for two more weeks
   (D) To suggest that the librarian does not know the rules

Purpose Questions

Listen to **Track 1.19**. Take notes using the template below as you listen to the conversation.

Key Terms
- collies
- poodles
- dog intelligence

Vocabulary
- **dog breeds (n):** the various types of dogs; two examples of dog breeds are the poodle and the chow chow
- **respectively (adv):** in that order

Things to Consider

WHY are the speakers having the conversation?

Notes
_____
_____
_____

Answer the following multiple-choice questions.

7) Why does the student visit the professor?
   (A) To talk about a Canadian researcher
   (B) To ask about studies on dog intelligence
   (C) To argue that dogs are smarter than humans
   (D) To ask the professor for dog-training tips

8) Listen to **Track 1.20**.
   Why does the student say this?
   (A) To prove that collies and poodles are the smartest dogs
   (B) To argue that dogs are not intelligent
   (C) To introduce a question with a personal experience
   (D) To explain why she likes dogs more than cats

Conversation Question Type 4: Inference

WHAT IS AN INFERENCE QUESTION?

Inference Questions may ask you to make an inference based on the information in the conversation, make a prediction about what a speaker will do after the conversation, or identify the speaker's attitude. Below are the three categories of inference questions that you might see on the conversation portion of the Listening test.

INFERENCE QUESTION FORMATS

Category 1 – Inference: An *inference* is a conclusion that is based on the facts of the conversation but not directly stated. In order to make an inference, you must pay attention to what the speaker suggests during a conversation. Common formats for **Inference Questions** include:

   What does the speaker imply/suggest about _____ in the conversation?
   What does the speaker mean when he/she says this?

Category 2 – Prediction: Prediction Questions ask you to identify what a speaker will do based on the information presented in the conversation. Thus, you must be able to infer a speaker's future actions based on what he or she says. Common formats for **Prediction Questions** include:

   What will the student probably do after talking to the professor/advisor?

Category 3 – Attitude: The speaker's attitude is his or her feelings about the information. For example, a speaker may express approval, disapproval, indifference, excitement, confusion, or surprise toward what is being discussed. Many times the speaker communicates an attitude indirectly. Common formats for **Attitude Questions** include:

   What is the speaker's opinion of _____?
   Which of the following best describes the speaker's attitude toward _____?

TIPS

Listening Tips: When listening for information that will help you make inferences and predictions, rely on your ability to find meanings that are "under" or "beneath" the speaker's words. Good notes may help you review what the speaker says.

Answer Tips: In questions about inferences, predictions, and attitudes, the correct answer will usually be stated indirectly. As such, these questions are much more difficult to answer than **Main Idea Questions, Detail Questions,** or **Purpose Questions.** When you encounter an **Inference,** a **Prediction,** or an **Attitude Question,** look at your notes if you cannot remember exactly what was said. Incorrect answer choices may:

- repeat the speaker's words with a different message
- be inaccurate based on what you hear in the conversation
- be irrelevant and not about anything mentioned in the conversation

Inference Questions

Listen to **Track 1.21**. Take notes using the template below as you listen to the conversation.

Key Terms
- double major
- physics
- history

Vocabulary
- "weigh my options" (idiom): consider which outcome is preferable
- consist of (phrasal verb): be made up of

Things to Consider

HOW do the speakers organize and present the conversation?
(Identify the speakers' attitudes and the implications of the conversation.)

Notes

stu. → advisor

stu. sounds nervous, unsure   wants to take unusual double major, FA says will be diff.

Answer the following multiple-choice questions.

Listen to **Track 1.22**.
What can be inferred from this statement?
(A) The student likes physics more than history.
(B) Not many students want to do double majors.
(C) The advisor has not heard of these major before.
(D) Not many students major in both physics and history.

What word best describes the student's attitude in this conversation?
(A) Confident
(B) Conflicted
(C) Fearful
(D) Overjoyed

Answer Explanation

Because physics is a science-related major and history is a humanities-related major, it is unusual for a student to major in both subjects. Based on this information, we can infer that the correct answer is **Choice D**.

Answer Explanation

Toward the end of the conversation, the student says that deciding whether or not to double major "is a very tough decision." Thus, we can infer that he feels conflicted, making the correct answer **Choice B**.

Inference Questions

Practice 1

Listen to **Track 1.23**. Take notes using the template below as you listen to the conversation.

Key Terms

singing in the bathroom
Paul Simon

Vocabulary

phenomenon (n): an event or action, usually with an unknown cause or origin

echo (v): when a sound is reflected and is heard after the original sound has stopped

Things to Consider

HOW do the speakers organize and present the conversation?
(Identify the speakers' attitudes and the implications of the conversation.)

Notes

_____
_____
_____

Answer the following multiple-choice questions.

1) What can be inferred about the student based on the conversation?
   (A) He enjoys singing in his free time.
   (B) He does not understand the professor.
   (C) He knows more about music than the professor does.
   (D) He wants to major in music history.

2) What is the professor's tone in the conversation?
   (A) Upset
   (B) Informative
   (C) Uncaring
   (D) Confused

Inference Questions

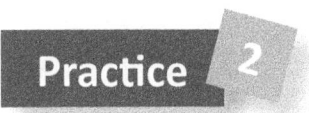

Listen to **Track 1.24**. Take notes using the template below as you listen to the conversation.

Key Terms
- final exam
- translate

Vocabulary
- "heads up" (idiom): warn someone in advance
- translate (v): convert from one language to another language

Things to Consider

HOW do the speakers organize and present the conversation?
(Identify the speakers' attitudes and the implications of the conversation.)

Notes
_____
_____
_____

Answer the following multiple-choice questions.

3) Listen to **Track 1.25**.
   Which word best describes the student's tone in this part of the conversation?
   (A) Anxious
   (B) Confused
   (C) Relieved
   (D) Angry

4) Listen to **Track 1.26**.
   What does the professor suggest when he says this?
   (A) He has not created the final exam yet.
   (B) He does not like creating final exams.
   (C) He has forgotten to create a final exam.
   (D) He has never created a final exam before.

Inference Questions

Practice 3

Listen to **Track 1.27**. Take notes using the template below as you listen to the conversation.

Key Terms
water pollution project
conclusion

Vocabulary
pollution (n): the existence of harmful substances in an environment
prediction (n): an educated guess

Things to Consider

HOW do the speakers organize and present the conversation?
(Identify the speakers' attitudes and the implications of the conversation.)

Notes
_____
_____
_____

Answer the following multiple-choice questions.

5) Listen to **Track 1.28**.
   Which word best describes the student's tone in this part of the conversation?
   (A) Persuasive
   (B) Frustrated
   (C) Furious
   (D) Overjoyed

6) What action will the student probably take regarding his project?
   (A) Give up on the project and drop the class
   (B) Retest all the water samples
   (C) Come up with a new topic for the project
   (D) Follow the professor's suggestions

Inference Questions

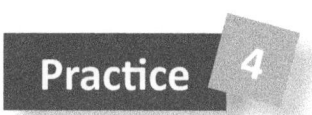

Listen to **Track 1.29**. Take notes using the template below as you listen to the conversation.

Key Terms
switch majors
head of the biology department
signature

Vocabulary
"walk you through" (idiom): guide someone through a process
signature (n): a distinct way of writing one's name so that it serves as a form of identification or authorization

Things to Consider

HOW do the speakers organize and present the conversation?
(Identify the speakers' attitudes and the implications of the conversation.)

Notes
_____
_____
_____

Answer the following multiple-choice questions.

7) What is the advisor's attitude during the conversation?
   (A) Supportive
   (B) Aggressive
   (C) Uncaring
   (D) Conflicted

8) What do you predict the student will do shortly after the conversation?
   (A) Reconsider her decision to switch majors
   (B) Talk to one of her sociology professors
   (C) Visit the head of the biology department
   (D) Go to another advisor for advice on switching majors

EXERCISE 1

As you listen to **Track 1.30**, take notes on the conversation between the university employee and the student. Then answer the multiple-choice questions that follow.

Key Terms

Music Appreciation 101
classical music CD
record store

Vocabulary

a buff (n): someone who is passionate and knowledgeable about a particular subject

Things to Consider

WHAT is the conversation about?

WHAT details contribute to the main idea?

WHY are the speakers having the conversation?

HOW do the speakers organize and present the conversation?
(Identify the speakers' attitudes and the implications of the conversation.)

Notes

_____
_____
_____
_____
_____
_____
_____
_____
_____
_____

EXERCISE 1

Circle the correct answer or answers to each of the multiple-choice questions below.

1) Where is this conversation taking place?
   (A) A computer store
   (B) A music class
   (C) A record store
   (D) A bookstore

2) What is the student looking for?
   (A) A textbook on music history
   (B) A classroom
   (C) A book of sheet music
   (D) A professor

3) What does the university employee recommend that the student do?
   (A) Talk to her professor
   (B) Go to the record store
   (C) Drop the class
   (D) Borrow his book

4) What can be inferred about the university employee?
   (A) He has worked the same job for many years.
   (B) He is not a student at the university.
   (C) He is knowledgeable about classical music.
   (D) He does not like the student.

5) How does the student feel at the end of the conversation?
   (A) Grateful
   (B) Frustrated
   (C) Confused
   (D) Anxious

EXERCISE 2

As you listen to **Track 1.31**, take notes on the conversation between the advisor and the man. Then answer the multiple-choice questions that follow.

Key Terms

- application
- Registrar's Office
- library

Vocabulary

registrar (n): a person who keeps the official records for a company or an organization

grove (n): a small group of trees

eligible (adj): meeting the requirements to do something

Things to Consider

WHAT is the conversation about?

WHAT details contribute to the main idea?

WHY are the speakers having the conversation?

HOW do the speakers organize and present the conversation?
(Identify the speakers' attitudes and the implications of the conversation.)

Notes

_____
_____
_____
_____
_____
_____
_____
_____
_____
_____

EXERCISE 2

Circle the correct answer or answers to each of the multiple-choice questions below.

1) Why is the man speaking to the advisor?
   (A) To receive some money
   (B) To apply to the university
   (C) To check out a book
   (D) To tour the campus

2) Where is this conversation taking place?
   (A) The Financial Aid Office
   (B) The library
   (C) The Registrar's Office
   (D) The Admissions Office

3) What does the advisor circle on the map?
   (A) The library
   (B) The Registrar's
   (C) The Financial Aid Office
   (D) The eucalyptus grove

4) Listen to **Track 1.32**.
   What does the man imply about the university when he says this?
   (A) Its academics are difficult.
   (B) Its layout is great.
   (C) It is crowded.
   (D) It is expensive.

5) What will the man probably do next?
   (A) Fill out an application
   (B) Study for a class
   (C) Walk north
   (D) Go home

EXERCISE 3

As you listen to **Track 1.33**, take notes on the conversation between the university employee and the student. Then answer the multiple choice questions that follow.

Key Terms

student ID

Vocabulary

discourage (v): influence someone not to do something

"learn my lesson" (idiom): learn something new through an unpleasant situation

Things to Consider

WHAT is the conversation about?

WHAT details contribute to the main idea?

WHY are the speakers having the conversation?

HOW do the speakers organize and present the conversation?
(Identify the speakers' attitudes and the implications of the conversation.)

Notes

_____
_____
_____
_____
_____
_____
_____
_____
_____
_____
_____
_____

EXERCISE 3

Circle the correct answer or answers to each of the multiple-choice questions below.

1) Why does the student go to see the university employee?
   (A) He needs to borrow 15 dollars.
   (B) His name is misspelled on his student ID.
   (C) He lost his student ID and needs a new one.
   (D) He wants to return a lost student ID card.

2) Listen to **Track 1.34**.
   What does the student imply when he says this?
   (A) He thinks that the university employee is joking.
   (B) He thinks that student IDs should be larger.
   (C) He did not know that the student IDs were made of plastic.
   (D) He thinks that the new student ID is too expensive.

3) What does the student need to present in order to receive a new student ID?
   Choose 2 answers.
   (A) A picture identification
   (B) Proof of insurance
   (C) 15 dollars
   (D) A piece of plastic

4) Why does the university charge 15 dollars to replace a student ID?
   (A) To pay for the materials used to print the student ID
   (B) To keep students from losing their student IDs
   (C) To help the school keep its tuition prices low
   (D) To help pay for the university employee's salary

5) What will the student probably do after talking to the university employee?
   (A) Try to find his lost student ID
   (B) Continue talking to the university employee
   (C) Get on the bus to go to class
   (D) Get his driver's license and money from his room

EXERCISE 4

As you listen to **Track 1.35**, take notes on the conversation between the professor and the student. Then answer the multiple-choice questions that follow.

Key Terms

lab internship
letter of recommendation

Vocabulary

competition (n): opposition, a person or people against whom one competes

spectroscopy (n): research regarding the range of colors that are produced when matter and radiation interact

Things to Consider

WHAT is the conversation about?

WHAT details contribute to the main idea?

WHY are the speakers having the conversation?

HOW do the speakers organize and present the conversation?
(Identify the speakers' attitudes and the implications of the conversation.)

Notes

_____
_____
_____
_____
_____
_____
_____
_____
_____
_____
_____

EXERCISE 4

Circle the correct answer or answers to each of the multiple-choice questions below.

1) Why does the student visit her professor?
   (A) To apply for a laboratory internship
   (B) To ask for a letter of recommendation
   (C) To ask about laboratory procedures
   (D) To ask about extra credit opportunities

2) What is the professor's opinion regarding summer lab internships?
   (A) They often lead to full-time lab jobs.
   (B) They are taught by inexperienced professors.
   (C) They tend to confuse students.
   (D) They are often very helpful.

3) On what day will the student's letter of recommendation be ready?
   (A) Monday
   (B) Tuesday
   (C) Wednesday
   (D) Thursday

4) What can be inferred about the student?
   (A) She is planning to go to medical school.
   (B) She has worked hard in her classes.
   (C) She does not have very good grades.
   (D) She has asked the professor for letters of recommendation before.

5) What is the professor's opinion of the work that the lab will do this summer?
   (A) It will probably be interesting.
   (B) It might be boring.
   (C) It should be difficult.
   (D) It is likely to be important.

EXERCISE 5

As you listen to **Track 1.36**, take notes on the conversation between the university employee and the student. Then answer the multiple-choice questions that follow.

Key Terms

Internet access
repair person

Vocabulary

depend on (phrasal verb): is determined by
solve (v): find an answer, find a way to fix an issue

Things to Consider

WHAT is the conversation about?

WHAT details contribute to the main idea?

WHY are the speakers having the conversation?

HOW do the speakers organize and present the conversation?
(Identify the speakers' attitudes and the implications of the conversation.)

Notes

_____
_____
_____
_____
_____
_____
_____
_____
_____
_____
_____

EXERCISE 5

Circle the correct answer or answers to each of the multiple-choice questions below.

1) Why does the student go to see the university employee?
   (A) To see if the library has Internet access
   (B) To apply for a job as an Internet repair person
   (C) To tell her that he cannot access the Internet
   (D) To restore the university's Internet access

2) What steps has the student already taken?
   Choose 2 answers.
   (A) He has searched for an Internet connection elsewhere on campus.
   (B) He has asked other students in his dormitory about the Internet.
   (C) He has spoken to an Internet repair person.
   (D) He has restarted his computer.

3) Listen to **Track 1.37**.
   Why does the student say this?
   (A) To explain his sense of urgency
   (B) To complain about a difficult class
   (C) To explain why he is staying up late
   (D) To explain that the situation will affect his report card

4) How does the university employee help the student?
   (A) She directs him to another department.
   (B) She says that she will check the Internet.
   (C) She promises to contact a repair person.
   (D) She suggests that he try connecting again.

5) What does the university employee imply about the library?
   (A) Its Internet connection is slow but reliable.
   (B) It is a convenient place to write reports.
   (C) Students always go there when the power is out.
   (D) It has lots of academic books and magazines.

TOEFL PATTERN LISTENING 1

CHAPTER 2

Academic Lectures

Chapter 2
Academic Lectures

EXPLANATION OF TASK

Each iBT TOEFL Listening section will include four to six academic lectures. These lectures will discuss topics that you are likely to encounter as a student at an American university. The topics are drawn from a range of academic fields, including psychology, biology, chemistry, the social sciences, and literature.

Each lecture is 3 to 5 minutes long. Because these lectures are supposed to replicate natural-sounding speech in an American university setting, the speakers may use English speech patterns such as repetition, digression from the main topic, false starts, pauses, and fillers (um, uh, eh, well). You will hear each lecture only once, but you are encouraged to take notes on the lecture information as you listen.

After you have listened to the lecture, you must answer six multiple-choice questions that relate to the lecture information. These questions will be related to the main idea, purpose, organization, or implications of the lecture. You may use your notes when answering the questions.

 Because this is the introductory-level book in the series, the conversations in this book are shorter and use simpler language than those you will encounter on the iBT TOEFL.

LECTURE FORMAT

The excerpt that you listen to will likely be of a professor lecturing on a certain subject. However, you may also hear an excerpt of a professor answering a student's question, or a back-and-forth discussion between a professor and his or her students.

NECESSARY SKILLS

In order to successfully complete the academic lecture portions of the Listening section, you must be able to:

- comprehend vocabulary regarding a variety of academic topics
- take notes on academic material
- summarize spoken information
- recognize the main idea and details of a spoken academic lecture
- determine the purpose of a spoken academic lecture
- make inferences about the organization and content of a spoken academic lecture
- make inferences about the attitude of the speaker

Question Types

The iBT TOEFL Listening section consists of four main types of questions.

1 Main Idea Questions

Main Idea Questions will require you to identify the main topic of the lecture. Because the answers to these questions are drawn directly from the lecture content, taking notes may guide you when answering these questions.

2 Detail Questions

Detail Questions will require you to identify a detail, an example, or an explanation related to the main topic. Because the answers to these questions are drawn directly from the lecture content, taking notes may guide you when answering these questions.

3 Purpose Questions

Purpose Questions will require you to identify *why* the speaker makes a particular statement or asks a particular question. Therefore, when listening to the lecture, concentrate on fully comprehending the purpose of the lecture.

4 Inference Questions

Inference Questions will require you to make an inference, or assumption, based on the contents of the lecture. An inference question might ask you to identify the speaker's tone or the lecture's basic structure.

Academic Lecture Question Type 1: Main Idea

WHAT IS A MAIN IDEA QUESTION?

The *main idea*, or topic, is the overall subject of the lecture. Use caution when answering **Main Idea Questions**: the lecturer will not always directly state his main idea. Therefore, you may have to infer the main idea based on the details and examples provided by the speaker. There will be one **Main Idea Question** after each academic lecture.

HOW TO TAKE NOTES

When taking notes on an academic lecture, the main idea will likely be one of the first things you write down. As you listen to the lecture, ask yourself, "**WHAT** is the lecture about?" Doing so will make identifying and answering the **Main Idea Question** easier.

MAIN IDEA QUESTION FORMATS

Main Idea Questions will usually ask you to identify the main idea, subject, or topic of the lecture. Common formats for a **Main Idea Question** include:

What is the main topic of the lecture?
What is the main purpose of the lecture?
What is the lecture mainly about?
What is the professor discussing in the lecture?

TIPS

Listening Tips: When listening for **Main Idea Questions**, focus on information presented in the beginning of the lecture. This part of the lecture sometimes contains important words, phrases, and sentences that indicate the main idea of the lecture.

Answer Tips: In questions about the topic or main idea, the correct answer will deal with the general subject of the lecture. Incorrect answer choices may be:

- broader than the focus of the lecture
- details of the lecture, not the main idea
- erroneous according to the speaker
- about a subject not mentioned in the lecture

Main Idea Questions

Listen to **Track 2.01**. Take notes using the template below as you listen to the lecture.

Key Terms

graffiti

Vocabulary

convey (v): communicate a concept or idea
vandalism (n): the purposeful destruction of property

Things to Consider

WHAT is the lecture about?

Notes

graffiti = drawing/writing spray-painted on public space

some like (think it's art), most dislike (vandalism)

Answer the following multiple-choice question.

What is the lecture mainly about?

(A) People's changing opinions of art
(B) The best methods for preventing vandalism
(C) Different styles of street art found around the world
(D) A practice regarded as both artistic and destructive

Answer Explanation

The lecture contains the clauses "some people consider graffiti an art form," and "many people… consider graffiti to be an act of vandalism." This indicates that the main idea of the lecture is graffiti, or *a practice regarded as both artistic and destructive*. Thus, the correct answer is **choice D**.

Main Idea Questions

Listen to **Track 2.02**. Take notes using the template below as you listen to the lecture.

Key Terms
depression
sadness

Vocabulary
traumatic (adj): emotionally upsetting or harmful
gene (n): a segment of DNA that determines an organism's traits or behavior
abuse (n): the improper use or overuse of something

Things to Consider

WHAT is the lecture about?

Notes
_____
_____
_____
_____

Answer the following multiple-choice question.

1) What is the main topic of this lecture?
   (A) Common methods for treating clinical depression
   (B) The differences between sadness and depression
   (C) The causes of common mental illnesses
   (D) The rapid spread of depression among Americans

Main Idea Questions

Listen to **Track 2.03**. Take notes using the template below as you listen to the lecture.

Key Terms

flag
vexillum

Vocabulary

cavalry (n): soldiers who fought while riding horses
the Middle Ages (n): a period of European history, usually dated from the 5th to the 15th centuries

Things to Consider

WHAT is the lecture about?

Notes

_____
_____
_____

Answer the following multiple-choice question.

2) What does the lecture mainly discuss?

(A) The origins of flags in Europe

(B) The military history of Europe

(C) How the Roman military became so effective

(D) How Hollywood dramatizes western history

Main Idea Questions

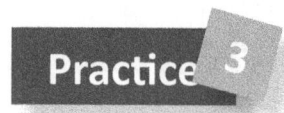

Listen to **Track 2.04**. Take notes using the template below as you listen to the lecture.

Key Terms
salt
salarium

Vocabulary
preservative (n): a substance used to prevent food or other materials from spoiling
commodity (n): a raw material that is traded
refer to (phrasal verb): describe, pertain to

Things to Consider
WHAT is the lecture about?

Notes
_____
_____
_____

Answer the following multiple-choice question.

3) What is the main topic of the lecture?
   (A) How ancient salt differed from modern salt
   (B) The harmful effects of a low-salt diet
   (C) The importance of salt in ancient times
   (D) Locations with large supplies of salt

Main Idea Questions

Listen to **Track 2.05**. Take notes using the template below as you listen to the lecture.

Key Terms
- diesel engine
- pressure
- compression chamber

Vocabulary
- efficient (adj): operating with as little wasted energy or effort as possible
- combust (v): burn, ignite

Things to Consider

WHAT is the lecture about?

Notes
_____
_____
_____

Answer the following multiple-choice question.

4) What is the main topic of the lecture?
   (A) The different types of engines used in automobiles
   (B) The ways that compression is used in engineering
   (C) The early history of steam and coal engines
   (D) The reasons that diesel engines are so efficient

Academic Lecture Question Type 2: Detail

WHAT IS A DETAIL QUESTION?

Details are specific pieces of information that relate to a larger topic. These pieces of information can be facts, descriptions, reasons, or examples. **Detail Questions** will ask you to recall specific information from the lecture as it was stated by the speaker. There will be one to three **Detail Questions** in each academic lecture.

HOW TO TAKE NOTES

When taking notes on an academic lecture, the details will likely be spread throughout the lecture. Focus on writing down only details that relate to the main idea of the lecture. **Before taking notes, try to identify the main idea of the lecture**.

As you listen to the lecture, ask yourself, "**WHAT** details contribute to the main idea?" Doing so will make identifying and answering the **Detail Questions** easier.

DETAIL QUESTION FORMATS

Detail Questions will ask you to identify specific details, explanations, or examples that relate to the main idea of the lecture. Common formats for the **Detail Questions** include:

> *What does the professor say about _____ in the lecture?*
> *According to the professor, what is true about _____?*
> *What is said about _____ in the lecture?*
> *Who/What/Where/When/Why/How _____?*

Whereas **Main Idea Questions** always appear as multiple-choice questions with one correct answer, **Detail Questions** have one, two, or three correct answer choices.

TIPS

Listening Tips: When listening for details, notice information that contributes to the main idea of the lecture. This information may involve information such as numbers, dates, names, definitions, reasons, connections, choices, and processes.

Answer Tips: In questions about details, the correct answer will always restate facts, descriptions, reasons, and examples from the lecture. When you answer detail questions, try to recall exactly what was said by the speaker. Look at your notes if you cannot remember exactly what was said. Incorrect answer choices may:

- repeat some of the speaker's words but convey a different meaning
- use words that sound like, but are actually different from, the speaker's words
- be inaccurate or irrelevant based on what you hear in the lecture

Detail Questions

Listen to **Track 2.06**. Take notes using the template below as you listen to the lecture. Then answer the multiple-choice questions that follow.

Key Terms
- philosophy
- moral philosopher
- natural philosopher

Vocabulary
- **ethics (n):** the study of the ways morals influence an individual's or group's actions and thoughts
- **specialist (n):** an individual who focuses on one area of study or one activity

Things to Consider
WHAT is the lecture about?

WHAT details contribute to the main idea?

Notes
phil. → used to be study of many subjects

In 19th c. → nat. phil. studied sciences, moral phil. studied ethics

Answer the following multiple-choice questions.

What modern subjects might a natural philosopher have studied?
(A) History and archaeology
(B) Ethics and political science
(C) Literature and linguistics
(D) Biology and chemistry

During the 19th century, what would a person who studied ethics have been called?
(A) An ethical expert
(B) A natural philosopher
(C) A moral philosopher
(D) A university student

Answer Explanation
Because the professor states that "all you biology and chemistry major would have been natural philosophers…" the correct answer must be **Choice D**.

Answer Explanation
The lecture states that a "specialists in ethics were called 'moral philosophers.'" Thus, the correct answer must be **Choice C**.

Detail Questions

Practice 1

Listen to **Track 2.07**. Take notes using the template below as you listen to the lecture.

Key Terms
- Georgia
- Atlanta
- economy

Vocabulary
- commercial (adj): having to do with trade or commerce
- financial (n): having to do with the supervision of money, usually in large amounts
- representative (adj): typical, characteristic

Things to Consider

WHAT is the lecture about?

WHAT details contribute to the main idea?

Notes

_____
_____
_____

Answer the following multiple-choice questions.

1) According to the professor, what feature makes Georgia an important state?
   (A) It contains many small towns and rural areas.
   (B) It has the largest city in the United States.
   (C) It is the wealthiest state in the United States.
   (D) It is an important area for manufacturing and business.

2) Which of the following characterize Atlanta?
   Choose 2 answers.
   (A) Georgia's largest city
   (B) Georgia's capital city
   (C) Georgia's oldest city
   (D) Georgia's noisiest city

Detail Questions

Listen to **Track 2.08**. Take notes using the template below as you listen to the lecture.

Key Terms
- banjo
- folk music
- Africa
- America

Vocabulary
- pluck (v): produce sound on a stringed instrument with one's fingers, strum
- distinctive (adj): describing a trait that separates or distinguishes one person or thing from others

Things to Consider

WHAT is the lecture about?

WHAT details contribute to the main idea?

Notes
_____
_____
_____

Answer the following multiple-choice questions.

3) Based on the lecture, the banjo is important to which type of music?
   (A) Traditional African music
   (B) American folk music
   (C) Classical music
   (D) Round drum music

4) According to the professor, what connection does Thomas Jefferson have to the banjo?
   (A) He played the instrument with his friends.
   (B) He made the banjo the national instrument.
   (C) He traveled through Africa searching for its origins.
   (D) He commented on the talent of black banjo players.

Detail Questions

Listen to **Track 2.09**. Take notes using the template below as you listen to the lecture.

Key Terms
- wasps
- farmers
- nectar
- pollinators

Vocabulary
- provoke (v): purposefully make someone or something angry

Things to Consider

WHAT is the lecture about?

WHAT details contribute to the main idea?

Notes

_____
_____
_____

Answer the following multiple-choice questions.

5) According to the professor, what qualities do most people associate with wasps?
   (A) They are easily angered and deliver painful stings.
   (B) They are harmful animals that destroy crops.
   (C) They are mysterious and solitary.
   (D) They are friendly and harmless.

6) In what ways are wasps considered helpful?
   Choose 2 answers.
   (A) They help scientists conduct eye research.
   (B) They only sting people who are mean.
   (C) They eat insects that are harmful to crops.
   (D) They feed on nectar and pollinate flowers.

Detail Questions

Listen to **Track 2.10**. Take notes using the template below as you listen to the lecture.

Key Terms
- public housing projects
- federal government
- income

Vocabulary
- vouchers (n): written promises by the government to pay for an individual's housing or schooling
- racial segregation (n): the separation of groups of people on the basis of race

Things to Consider

WHAT is the lecture about?

WHAT details contribute to the main idea?

Notes

_____
_____
_____

Answer the following multiple-choice questions.

7) What are the two main methods the U.S. federal government has used to house the poor?
   Choose 2 answers.
   (A) Developing new laws
   (B) Building public housing
   (C) Providing rent vouchers
   (D) Buying private apartments

8) What is one possible result of poor people living in privately owned apartments?
   (A) They may have more windows.
   (B) They may have more privacy.
   (C) They may save money.
   (D) They may find jobs more easily.

Academic Lecture Question Type 3: Purpose

WHAT IS A PURPOSE QUESTION?

The "purpose" of a statement is the speaker's intention; you must infer purpose based on what the speaker says. In some **Purpose Questions,** you will listen to part of the lecture again before answering. There are usually one or two **Purpose Questions** that accompany each academic lecture.

HOW TO TAKE NOTES

The speakers usually state their purpose early in the conversation and continue to imply it through what they say and ask. **When taking notes on the purpose of the lecture, try to quickly identify the main idea.**

As you listen to the conversation, ask yourself, "**WHY** did the speaker include this information?" Doing so will make identifying and answering **Purpose Questions** easier.

PURPOSE QUESTION FORMATS

Purpose Questions will usually ask you why the speaker made a certain claim. Common formats for **Purpose Questions** include:

Why does the professor explain _____?
Why does the professor ask the class about _____?
Why does the professor say this?
Why does the student ask/say _____?

TIPS

Listening Tips: When listening for the purpose of a lecture or statement, you must rely on your ability to draw logical conclusions to determine *why* a statement is being made. Your notes may help you piece information from the lecture together.

Answer Tips: The correct answers to **Purpose Questions** will often be stated indirectly. Thus, these questions are slightly more difficult to answer than **Main Idea** or **Detail Questions**. When answering **Purpose Questions**, look at your notes if you cannot remember exactly what the speakers said. Incorrect answer choices may:

- repeat some of the speaker's words but convey a different meaning
- use words that sound like but are actually different from the speaker's words
- be inaccurate based on what you hear in the lecture
- be irrelevant and not about anything mentioned in the lecture

Purpose Questions

Listen to **Track 2.11**. Take notes using the template below as you listen to the lecture.

Key Terms
marine sponges
various shapes and sizes

Vocabulary
textured (adj): having a raised, rough, or bumpy surface
species (n): a group of similar organisms capable of reproducing with one another

Things to Consider

WHY did the speaker present the lecture information?

Notes
variety of marine sponges → diff. sizes/shapes

purpose → get students interested in sponges

Answer the following multiple-choice questions.

Why does the speaker describe several different types of marine sponge?
(A) To warn students of dangerous marine sponges
(B) To illustrate that sponges vary in appearance and size
(C) To explain how sponges affect their environments
(D) To demonstrate why sponges are the oldest organisms in existence

Why does the speaker claim that some marine sponges are "smooth and hard, like rocks"?
(A) To describe the texture of some sponges
(B) To show that some sponges cling to rocks
(C) To explain that sponges are heavy and immobile
(D) To suggest that some sponges are as durable as rocks

Answer Explanation
In the lecture, the professor emphasizes the fact that "marine sponges have various shapes and sizes." Because she gives examples of various sponges in the rest of the lecture, the correct answer must be **Choice B**.

Answer Explanation
The lecture states that some sponges are "smooth and hard, like rocks." The lecturer is comparing sponges to rocks to describe sponges' texture, so the correct answer must be **Choice A**.

Purpose Questions

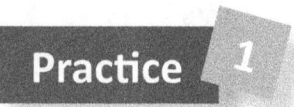

Listen to **Track 2.12**. Take notes using the template below as you listen to the lecture.

Key Terms
- coffee
- caffeine

Vocabulary
- stimulate (v): raise levels of activity
- component (n): a part or fraction of a whole thing
- therapeutic (adj): having to do with healing or curing an illness

Things to Consider

WHY did the speaker present the lecture information?

Notes
_____
_____
_____

Answer the following multiple-choice questions.

1) Why does the professor mention coffee at the beginning of the lecture?
   (A) To argue that coffee is better than tea
   (B) To introduce the topic of heated beverages
   (C) To warn students about the dangerous, caffeinated beverage
   (D) To discuss the chemical effects of coffee

2) Listen to **Track 2.13**.
   Why does the professor say this?
   (A) To explain a potential side effect of drinking coffee
   (B) To prove that coffee is a harmful substance
   (C) To address a student's question
   (D) To provide an explanation for a mysterious phenomenon

Purpose Questions

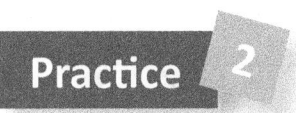

Listen to **Track 2.14**. Take notes using the template below as you listen to the lecture.

Key Terms
African elephant
Asian elephant

Vocabulary
tusk (n): a long, pointed tooth that usually sticks out of an animal's mouth, as in boars and elephants
interbreed (v): breed two animals that belong to different species
crossbreed (n): an animal produced by interbreeding

Things to Consider
WHY did the speaker present the lecture information?

Notes
_____
_____
_____

Answer the following multiple-choice questions.

3) Why does the professor mention African and Asian elephants' ears?
   (A) To explain why elephants are often hunted
   (B) To describe a difference between Asian and African elephants
   (C) To explain how African elephants hear so well
   (D) To point out the most noticeable characteristic of Asian elephants

4) Why does the professor mention the attempt to crossbreed an African and an Asian elephant?
   (A) To emphasize the genetic differences between Asian and African elephants
   (B) To show that most newborn elephants are very unhealthy
   (C) To show support for further research into elephant interbreeding
   (D) To explain the primary difference between male and female elephants

Purpose Questions

Listen to **Track 2.15**. Take notes using the template below as you listen to the lecture.

Key Terms
- daylight savings
- Benjamin Franklin
- Time Act of 1966

Vocabulary
- annual (adj): yearly, happening every year,

Things to Consider

WHY did the speaker present the lecture information?

Notes
_____
_____
_____

Answer the following multiple-choice questions.

5) Why does the professor mention Benjamin Franklin in the lecture?
   (A) To name someone who opposed daylight savings
   (B) To explain the origins of daylight savings
   (C) To link daylight savings to American wars
   (D) To explain the background of the Uniform Time Act

6) Listen to **Track 2.16**.
   Why does the professor say this?
   (A) To share a personal experience related to daylight savings
   (B) To express his disapproval of daylight savings time
   (C) To explain how daylight savings influenced his choice of profession
   (D) To predict the future of daylight savings in the U.S.

Purpose Questions

Listen to **Track 2.17**. Take notes using the template below as you listen to the lecture.

Key Terms

Ancient Greek theaters
acoustics
orchestra

Vocabulary

bleachers (n): outdoor seating, usually used while viewing a concert or sports game
terraced (adj): being composed of step-like levels

Things to Consider

WHY did the speaker present the lecture information?

Notes

_____
_____
_____

Answer the following multiple-choice questions.

7) Why does the professor discuss Greek theaters?
   (A) To introduce an ancient Greek play to the class
   (B) To show how ancient Greek theaters influenced Greek politics
   (C) To contrast ancient Greek theaters with modern theaters
   (D) To describe the unique features of ancient Greek theaters

8) Listen to **Track 2.18**.
   Why does the professor say this?
   (A) To emphasize the hugeness of Greek theaters
   (B) To explain how sound travels in most structures
   (C) To show how clear the acoustics in a Greek theater are
   (D) To demonstrate why Greek theater remains popular today

Academic Lecture Question Type 4: Inference

WHAT IS AN INFERENCE QUESTION?

Inference Questions may ask you to make an inference based on the information in the lecture, explain the organization of the lecture, or identify the speaker's attitude. Below are the four categories of inference questions that you might see on the lecture portion of the Listening test.

INFERENCE QUESTION FORMATS

Category 1 – Inference: An *inference* is a conclusion drawn from material but that is not directly stated. In order to make an inference, you must pay attention to what the speaker suggests during a lecture. Common formats for **Inference Questions** include:

What can be inferred about _____ in the lecture?
What does the professor imply/suggest about _____ in the lecture?
What does the professor mean by this statement?

Category 2 – Organization: Organization Questions ask you to identify the order in which the lecture information is presented. Thus, **Organization Questions** ask you how the speaker presents the information, for example, as a cause and effect. Common formats for **Organization Questions** include:

How does the speaker organize the lecture information?
How does the speaker clarify the points he/she made about _____?

Category 3 – Attitude: The speaker's attitude is his or her feelings about the information. For example, a speaker may feel approval, disapproval, indifference, excitement, confusion, or surprise toward what is being discussed. Many times the speaker communicates an attitude indirectly.
Common formats for **Attitude Questions** include:

What is the professor's opinion of _____?
What is the professor's attitude toward _____?

Category 4 – Connecting Information: Some lectures will include a Connecting Information Chart. To complete it, you must be able to categorize information presented in the lecture. Thus, you must understand the lecture's main idea and details to complete these charts.

TIPS

Answer Tips: In questions about inferences, organization, and attitude, the correct answer will usually be given indirectly. As such, these questions are more difficult to answer than **Main Idea**, **Detail**, and **Purpose Questions**. When you answer **Inference Questions**, look at your notes if you cannot remember exactly what was said. Incorrect answer choices may:

- repeat the speaker's words with a different message
- be inaccurate based on what you hear in the lecture
- be irrelevant and not about anything mentioned in the lecture

Inference Questions

Listen to **Track 2.19**. Take notes using the template below as you listen to the lecture.

Key Terms
- cats
- domestication
- grain harvests

Vocabulary
- **domesticated (adj):** tamed from the wild
- **revere (v):** honor, greatly respect
- **ferret (n):** a small mammal that can be trained to catch mice and rats

Things to Consider

HOW does the speaker organize and present the lecture?
(Identify the organization methods, tone, and implications of the speaker.)

Notes

org.: grain cultures loved cats, cat gods (eat mice) except one—Greek

Greek cats = moon/world of dead

implied: Greek view diff. (had ferrets)

Answer the following multiple-choice questions.

What can be concluded about Greek culture based on the information in the lecture?
(A) Only Greeks associated cats with the moon.
(B) Greeks did not keep large stores of grain.
(C) Greeks used ferrets to fight off wild cats.
(D) Greeks did not use cats to catch mice.

How does the professor clarify the idea that "ancient Greeks had an unusual attitude about cats"?
(A) She explains cats' lesser role in Greek religion.
(B) She describes the roots of modern beliefs about cats.
(C) She discusses cat deities in China, India, and Egypt.
(D) She provides examples of cat domestication.

Answer Explanation

This is an **Inference Question**. The lecture states that, while many ancient cultures revered cats for protecting grain and books from mice, the ancient Greeks "had pet ferrets to catch mice." Greeks used ferrets, not cats, to catch mice, so we can conclude that the correct answer must be **Choice D**.

Answer Explanation

This is an **Organization Question**. Because the lecture suggests that most ancient cultures revered cats as deities, but points out that ancient Greek culture placed cats in a less powerful position, we can conclude that that the correct answer must be **Choice A**.

Inference Questions

Listen to **Track 2.20**. Take notes using the template below as you listen to the lecture.

Key Terms
- myth
- Mircea Eliade

Vocabulary
principle (n): a fact or idea that serves as the basis for a system of behaviors or beliefs

Things to Consider

HOW does the speaker organize and present the lecture?
(Identify the organization methods, tone, and implications of the speaker.)

Notes
_____
_____
_____

Answer the following multiple-choice questions.

1) What does the professor imply about myths in the lecture?
   (A) They no longer interest people in the modern world.
   (B) They are frequently used by writers of fiction books.
   (C) They are often literal statements of past history.
   (D) They contain more truth than most people realize.

2) Listen to **Track 2.21**.
   What does the professor mean when he says this?
   (A) He agrees with Mircea Eliade's view of myths.
   (B) He is knowledgeable about Mircea Eliade.
   (C) He once studied with Mircea Eliade.
   (D) He has trouble explaining Mircea Eliade's ideas.

Inference Questions

Listen to **Track 2.22**. Take notes using the template below as you listen to the lecture.

Key Terms
American literature
plantation
Southern colonies

Vocabulary
pursuit (n): a specific activity that one undertakes
fruitful (adj): productive, creating much of something

Things to Consider

HOW does the speaker organize and present the lecture?
(Identify the organization methods, tone, and implications of the speaker.)

Notes
_____
_____
_____

Answer the following multiple-choice questions.

3) What does the professor suggest about the inhabitants of the Northern colonies in the lecture?

   Choose 2 answers.

   (A) They were generally more religious than Southern colonists.
   (B) They were much wealthier than the Southern colonists.
   (C) They envied the lifestyles of southern plantation owners.
   (D) They produced most of America's early literature.

4) Listen to **Track 2.23**.
   What does the author imply about the South when she says this?
   (A) It only produced literature about farming.
   (B) It relied heavily on fruit harvesting in the 19th and 20th centuries.
   (C) It experienced many natural disasters before the 19th and 20th centuries.
   (D) It produced many great writers during the 19th and 20th centuries.

Inference Questions

Practice 3

Listen to **Track 2.24**. Take notes using the template below as you listen to the lecture.

Key Terms

paleontologist   birds
dinosaurs   fossils
color vision

Vocabulary

paleontologist (n): a scientist who studies fossils
optic (adj): relating to eyes or vision
orient (v): find one's bearings or position

Things to Consider

HOW does the speaker organize and present the lecture?
(Identify the organization methods, tone, and implications of the speaker.)

Notes

_____
_____
_____

Answer the following multiple-choice questions.

5) How does the professor organize the lecture information?
   (A) He disproves a controversial theory using scientific evidence.
   (B) He presents theories that attempt to explain a main question.
   (C) He has students analyze the results of an experiment.
   (D) He asks students to disprove a popular theory.

6) Listen to **Track 2.25**.
   What does the professor mean when he says this?
   (A) Everyone wants to question the conclusions scientists make.
   (B) Most paleontologists believe dinosaurs had pretty eyes.
   (C) Asking scientific questions is similar to serving in a jury.
   (D) Paleontologists are uncertain whether or not dinosaurs saw color.

Inference Questions

Practice 4

Listen to **Track 2.26**. Take notes using the template below as you listen to the lecture.

Key Terms
plastic
lightweight
strong
resistant to decay

Vocabulary
versatile (adj.): used for many different purposes

Things to Consider

HOW does the speaker organize and present the lecture?
(Identify the organization methods, tone, and implications of the speaker.)

Notes
_____
_____
_____

Answer the following multiple-choice questions.

7) What does the professor imply about plastic?
   (A) It decays when exposed to sunlight.
   (B) It is usually quite fragile.
   (C) It forms a durable material when heated.
   (D) It is necessary for everyday life.

8) Listen to **Track 2.27**.
   What does the professor imply when she says this?
   (A) Plastic-related research is among the most expensive scientific research.
   (B) Almost all scientists are involved in plastic-related research.
   (C) Plastics are used in many products for different industries.
   (D) Only scientists use plastics regularly.

EXERCISE 1

Take notes as you listen to the academic lecture on **Track 2.28**. Then answer the multiple-choice questions that follow.

Key Terms

vitamins
Vitamin C

Vocabulary

component (n): a part of a larger object, process, or idea
compound (n): a substance made of two or more elements

Things to Consider

WHAT is the lecture about?

WHAT details contribute to the main idea?

WHY does the speaker present the lecture information?

HOW does the speaker organize and present the lecture?

Notes

_____
_____
_____
_____
_____
_____
_____
_____
_____
_____

EXERCISE 1

Circle the correct answer or answers to each of the multiple-choice questions below.

1) What is the main topic of the lecture?
   (A) Some qualities of vitamins
   (B) The difficulty of finding the correct vitamins
   (C) Some benefits of consuming vitamins
   (D) The importance of Vitamin C

2) Listen to **Track 2.29**.
   Why does the professor say this in response to the student's answer?
   (A) To tell the student to shorten his response
   (B) To suggest that more students should answer the question
   (C) To demonstrate that the question is very difficult to answer
   (D) To confirm that the student's response was mostly correct

3) According to the professor, what is a vitamin?
   (A) A compound that damages the environment
   (B) A substance only produced by humans
   (C) A compound that is not produced by the body
   (D) A substance that causes illness in some people

4) What does the professor say about Vitamin C?
   (A) Most organisms naturally produce it.
   (B) It is the most plentiful vitamin.
   (C) It is only produced in plants.
   (D) It was the first vitamin to be discovered.

5) Which of the following organisms needs to consume Vitamin C in order to survive?
   (A) Plants
   (B) Humans
   (C) Dogs
   (D) Whales

6) What will the professor probably talk about next?
   (A) The most common types of vitamins
   (B) The history of vitamin-related research
   (C) The potential dangers of taking vitamins
   (D) The functions of vitamins in the body

EXERCISE 2

Take notes as you listen to the academic lecture on **Track 2.30**. Then answer the multiple-choice questions that follow.

Key Terms

Adam Smith   bargaining
economics   conspire
efficient

Vocabulary

bargain (v): discuss the conditions in which a person will buy or sell something

conspire (v): make harmful or illegal plans with others in secret

Things to Consider

WHAT is the lecture about?

WHAT details contribute to the main idea?

WHY does the speaker present the lecture information?

HOW does the speaker organize and present the lecture?

Notes

___
___
___
___
___
___
___
___
___
___
___

EXERCISE 2

Circle the correct answer or answers to each of the multiple-choice questions below.

1) What is the main topic of this lecture?
   (A) Basic arguments in the field of economics
   (B) Advice for economic advisors
   (C) A biography of the father of economics
   (D) A brief introduction to Adam Smith's theories

2) What does the professor imply about Smith's opinion of bargaining?
   (A) Smith encouraged it.
   (B) Smith hated it.
   (C) Smith thought that it should be controlled by the government.
   (D) Smith did not address this topic.

3) Why does the professor mention a shoemaker?
   (A) To describe a chapter in Smith's book
   (B) To give an example of something supported by Smith
   (C) To give details of 18th-century markets
   (D) To emphasize the importance of shoemakers in a large market

4) Why does Smith use the metaphor of the "invisible hand"?
   (A) To refer to government officials
   (B) To explain religion's role in economics
   (C) To discuss free and fair markets
   (D) To describe money

5) Listen to **Track 2.31**.
   Why does the professor say this?
   (A) To explain an additional argument
   (B) To criticize other professors
   (C) To correct a common misconception
   (D) To add details to the preceding statement

6) Which of the following describes Adam Smith's view of government?
   (A) It should oversee markets.
   (B) It must avoid taxing people.
   (C) It should control prices.
   (D) It should help farmers.

EXERCISE 3

Take notes as you listen to the academic lecture on **Track 2.32**. Then answer the multiple-choice questions that follow.

Key Terms

mass   gravity
weight   matter

Vocabulary

interchangeable (adj): identical, the same
matter (n): generally speaking, something that occupies space

Things to Consider

WHAT is the lecture about?

WHAT details contribute to the main idea?

WHY does the speaker present the lecture information?

HOW does the speaker organize and present the lecture?

Notes

_____
_____
_____
_____
_____
_____
_____
_____
_____
_____
_____

EXERCISE 3

Circle the correct answer or answers to each of the multiple-choice questions below.

1) What does the professor mainly discuss?
   (A) Important equations used in physics
   (B) Terms that are interchangeable
   (C) The different meanings of words in physics
   (D) The difference between "mass" and "weight"

2) What does the professor say about the use of the terms "mass" and "weight" in everyday speech?
   (A) They are difficult terms for many people to understand.
   (B) They are often used interchangeably.
   (C) They have different meanings depending on context.
   (D) They are usually used correctly.

3) Listen to **Track 2.33**.
   Why does the professor mention "anything you can touch"?
   (A) To encourage students to become involved
   (B) To explain the meaning of weight
   (C) To describe a general characteristic of objects with mass
   (D) To point out the reason for finding an object's mass

4) How does the professor explain the term "weight"?
   (A) He gives an example about traveling in a spaceship.
   (B) He shows the class a short video.
   (C) He describes the experiences of various astronauts.
   (D) He supports his point with facts and numbers.

5) Why would the professor be able to float around in a spaceship?
   (A) Without gravity, he would weigh the same as air.
   (B) Without gravity, he would have more strength.
   (C) A space ship could resist gravity and fly very fast.
   (D) As his muscle mass declined, he would be lighter.

6) Which of the following statements are true of mass?
   (A) An object's mass cannot be measured.
   (B) An object's mass decreases as its weight increases.
   (C) An object's mass is always equal to its weight.
   (D) An object's mass does not change based on location.

EXERCISE 4

Take notes as you listen to the academic lecture on **Track 2.34**. Then answer the multiple-choice questions that follow.

Key Terms

phantom limb syndrome
phantom limb pain

Vocabulary

amputee (n): a person whose limb(s) has been cut off or otherwise removed

Things to Consider

WHAT is the lecture about?

WHAT details contribute to the main idea?

WHY does the speaker present the lecture information?

HOW does the speaker organize and present the lecture?

Notes

_____
_____
_____
_____
_____
_____
_____
_____
_____
_____
_____

EXERCISE 4

Circle the correct answer or answers to each of the multiple-choice questions below.

1) What does the professor mainly discuss?
   (A) Mysteries involving phantoms
   (B) Medical progress in reattaching limbs
   (C) Some personal feelings
   (D) An unexplained physical sensation

2) Listen to **Track 2.35**.
   Why does the professor say this?
   (A) To talk about what people once believed
   (B) To describe the opposite of phantom limb syndrome
   (C) To clarify how she is using the term "phantom"
   (D) To show how frightening the syndrome is

3) What evidence does the professor give that supports the existence of phantom limb syndrome?
   (A) Medical researchers know what causes the syndrome.
   (B) The syndrome occurs no matter which limb is amputated.
   (C) Patients feel something that is not there.
   (D) Up to 80% of amputees experience it.

4) When does phantom limb syndrome become a medical concern?
   (A) When a patient complains of phantom limb pain
   (B) When a patient first notices the symptoms
   (C) When it is difficult to discover the cause of the syndrome
   (D) When doctors identify the phantom limb

5) How does the professor organize the lecture?
   (A) She describes phantom limb syndrome and then phantom limb pain.
   (B) She argues that phantom limb syndrome is fake.
   (C) She discusses the history of phantom limb pain.
   (D) She encourages students to discuss their phantom limb pains.

6) Where does the professor imply that the cause of phantom limb syndrome may be found?
   (A) In the spine
   (B) In the brain
   (C) In the joints
   (D) In the skin

EXERCISE 5

Take notes as you listen to the academic lecture on **Track 2.36**. Then answer the multiple-choice questions that follow.

Key Terms

William Seward
Alaska Purchase
Russia

Vocabulary

territory (n): an area of land owned by an individual, a state, or a nation
petroleum (n): liquid found underground that is used for the production of gasoline and oil
negotiate (v): reach an agreement

Things to Consider

WHAT is the lecture about?

WHAT details contribute to the main idea?

WHY does the speaker present the lecture information?

HOW does the speaker organize and present the lecture?

Notes

_____
_____
_____
_____
_____
_____
_____
_____
_____
_____
_____

EXERCISE 5

Circle the correct answer or answers to each of the multiple-choice questions below.

1) What is the lecture mainly about?
   (A) Russia's rulers in the 1800s
   (B) How and why Alaska became part of the U.S.
   (C) Whether or not buying Alaska was wise
   (D) The history of the native Alaskan people

2) Why did some Americans oppose the Alaska Purchase at first?
   (A) They thought the territory was too big.
   (B) They were depressed after the Civil War.
   (C) They wanted the U.S. to rebuild its own country.
   (D) They thought that the territory was too cold.

3) What does the professor imply about American attitudes toward Alaska?
   (A) Once the land became profitable, opponents changed their minds.
   (B) Attitudes did not change in spite of gold and oil discoveries.
   (C) Most Americans think of Alaska as a wealthy place.
   (D) Attitudes towards Alaska are constantly changing.

4) Why does the professor mention that, during the Seward Purchase, Canada belonged to the British?
   (A) To illustrate the importance of British colonies at the time
   (B) To imply that Russia and Britain were allies
   (C) To criticize the British government
   (D) To explain why Russia decided to sell Alaska

5) According to the professor, why were Russian rulers worried about owning Alaska?
   (A) It did not seem very useful to them.
   (B) They thought it would be difficult to protect.
   (C) They were afraid that few Russians would move there.
   (D) They had difficulty getting ships there safely.

6) What can be inferred from the lecture about Russia and the U.S. in 1867?
   (A) The two countries distrusted each other.
   (B) They were both powerful.
   (C) They wanted to stop British expansion.
   (D) They had both fought civil wars.

CHAPTER 3

Actual Practices

TOEFL PATTERN LISTENING 1

ACTUAL PRACTICE 1

Take notes as you listen to the lecture on **Track 3.01**. Then answer the multiple-choice questions that follow.

Design

- modernist design
- mass-produced
- Bauhaus
- wallpaper
- Marcel Breuer
- armchair
- bent metal tubes

Things to Consider

WHAT is the lecture about?

WHAT details contribute to the main idea?

WHY does the speaker present the lecture information?

HOW does the speaker organize and present the lecture?

Notes

_____
_____
_____
_____
_____
_____
_____
_____

Circle the letter next to the correct answer or answers to each of the multiple-choice questions below.

1) What is the main topic of the lecture?
   (A) The first art school in Germany
   (B) Art and design in the 20th century
   (C) The connection between bicycles and modernist design
   (D) One highly influential school for modernist designs

2) Where did the Bauhaus style originate?
   (A) The Netherlands
   (B) Germany
   (C) The United States
   (D) Spain

3) Based on the lecture, what did modernist designers probably believe?
   (A) Industrialization could lead to a better society.
   (B) Hand-crafted items have the most artistic value.
   (C) All art should be used for home decoration.
   (D) Most people did not like their furniture designs.

4) Listen to **Track 3.02**.
   What can be inferred about modernist designers from this?
   (A) Their furniture was meant for decoration, not for use.
   (B) Very few of them had any artistic training.
   (C) They only designed furniture from metal.
   (D) Their art was sometimes inspired by everyday objects.

5) What is the professor's general tone regarding the Bauhaus school's designs?
   (A) Critical
   (B) Humorous
   (C) Respectful
   (D) Promotional

6) What is the professor most likely to discuss next?
   (A) Current-day museum exhibits of Bauhaus products
   (B) Design schools that drew inspiration from the Bauhaus school
   (C) The design principles used in building steel-frame armchairs
   (D) The number of students at the Bauhaus school

Take notes as you listen to the conversation on **Track 3.03**. Then answer the multiple-choice questions that follow.

Daily Tribune Newspaper   interview
internship   writing samples
Dr. Henry

Things to Consider

WHAT is the conversation about?

WHAT details contribute to the main idea?

WHY are the speakers having the conversation?

HOW do the speakers organize and present the conversation?

Notes

_____
_____
_____
_____
_____
_____
_____
_____

Circle the letter next to the correct answer or answers to each of the multiple-choice questions below.

1) Where does the employee work?
   (A) An internship office
   (B) A career center
   (C) A newspaper publisher
   (D) A theater

2) Why is the student interested in the internship?
   (A) To explore a future career
   (B) To make money for college
   (C) To meet interesting people
   (D) To fulfill a school requirement

3) What subject does the student study at the university?
   (A) Journalism
   (B) English
   (C) Management
   (D) Creative Writing

4) Why does the student need to see Dr. Henry?
   (A) To fill out an application
   (B) To be interviewed
   (C) To enroll in a class
   (D) To learn about the woman

5) What does the employee ask the student to bring to his interview?
   (A) An application
   (B) A pen and pencil
   (C) Writing samples
   (D) A professor's recommendation

ACTUAL PRACTICE 1

Take notes as you listen to the lecture on **Track 3.04**. Then answer the multiple-choice questions that follow.

History

- button
- prehistoric
- fasten
- 13th-century Europe
- reinforced buttonhole
- Industrial Revolution

Things to Consider

WHAT is the lecture about?

WHAT details contribute to the main idea?

WHY does the speaker present the lecture information?

HOW does the speaker organize and present the lecture?

Notes

_____
_____
_____
_____
_____
_____
_____
_____

Circle the letter next to the correct answer or answers to each of the multiple-choice questions below.

1) What is the main subject of the lecture?
   (A) How buttons have affected fashion throughout history
   (B) The hobby of button collecting
   (C) The clothing styles of prehistoric Europe
   (D) The differences between men and women's clothing

2) From what substance might one of the first buttons have been made?
   (A) Gold or silver
   (B) Bone or wood
   (C) Ivory or marble
   (D) Plastic or cloth

3) Why did people begin using buttons instead of belts or pins?
   (A) To stop them from being hurt by pins
   (B) To make them appear more attractive
   (C) To fasten clothing more effectively
   (D) To keep them warmer in winter

4) What can be inferred about the shape of the first factory-made buttons?
   (A) It was more varied, including circles, squares, and triangles.
   (B) It was much bigger than today's buttons.
   (C) It was unpopular and became rare.
   (D) It was so popular that it remains the standard flat shape.

5) Put the following events in the correct historical order.

   > Arrange the historical events listed below in chronological order (from earliest to most recent). Use each event only once.

   (A) Cheaper buttons allow many people to wear tight clothing.
   (B) Hand-made buttons allow wealthy people to wear clothing that fits tightly on top.
   (C) People use seashell, bone, or wooden buttons for decoration only.
   (D) Factories begin to make buttons in larger numbers.

1)	
2)	
3)	
4)	

Take notes as you listen to the lecture on **Track 3.05**. Then answer the multiple-choice questions that follow.

Music Composition

- fugue
- subject melody
- answer melody
- exposition
- developmental episodes

Things to Consider

WHAT is the lecture about?

WHAT details contribute to the main idea?

WHY does the speaker present the lecture information?

HOW does the speaker organize and present the lecture?

Notes

_____
_____
_____
_____
_____
_____
_____
_____

Circle the letter next to the correct answer or answers to each of the multiple-choice questions below.

1) What is the main topic of the discussion?
   (A) An unsolved mystery in classical music history
   (B) A group of instruments no longer used today
   (C) A popular classical music composer
   (D) A type of classical music composition

2) What instrument played the "subject" melody in the fugue?
   (A) A flute
   (B) A cello
   (C) A violin
   (D) A piano

3) What does the professor say about the "answer" melodies in the fugue?
   (A) They are played in a different key.
   (B) They are supposed to make listeners laugh.
   (C) They are repeated five times.
   (D) They are quieter than the "subject" melody.

4) What can be inferred about the structure of a fugue from the lecture?
   (A) Musicians are encouraged to improvise their parts.
   (B) The melody is only played by one instrument.
   (C) The subject melody always comes after the answer melody.
   (D) The melody will change as different instruments play it.

5) Why does the professor question her students throughout the lecture?
   (A) To prepare them for an upcoming oral exam
   (B) To see if her students understand the lecture information
   (C) To grade them on their class participation
   (D) To understand why students are failing her class

6) What part of the fugue will the class discuss next?
   (A) The exposition
   (B) The developmental episodes
   (C) The conclusion
   (D) The counter-subject

Take notes as you listen to the conversation on **Track 3.06**. Then answer the multiple-choice questions that follow.

> report card   chemistry department
> Professor Keller   chemistry class

Things to Consider

WHAT is the conversation about?

WHAT details contribute to the main idea?

WHY are the speakers having the conversation?

HOW do the speakers organize and present the conversation?

Notes
_____
_____
_____
_____
_____
_____
_____
_____

Circle the letter next to the correct answer or answers to each of the multiple-choice questions below.

1) How does the man feel during the conversation?
   (A) Grateful
   (B) Upset
   (C) Excited
   (D) Curious

2) What grade did the woman get in the chemistry class?
   (A) A
   (B) B
   (C) C
   (D) F

3) What can be inferred about the man?
   (A) He lives off campus.
   (B) He once lived in Germany.
   (C) He is angry at the woman.
   (D) He knows a lot about chemistry.

4) What does the woman advise the male student to do?
   (A) Contact Professor Keller
   (B) Fly to Germany
   (C) Take chemistry again
   (D) Relax over winter break

5) What will the man do next?
   (A) Have a cup of coffee
   (B) Go to the chemistry department
   (C) Show the woman his report card
   (D) Change his major

Take notes as you listen to the lecture on **Track 3.07**. Then answer the multiple-choice questions that follow.

Psychology

conditioning
psychologists
Ivan Pavlov

John B. Watson
laboratory rat
association

Things to Consider

WHAT is the lecture about?

WHAT details contribute to the main idea?

WHY does the speaker present the lecture information?

HOW does the speaker organize and present the lecture?

Notes

Circle the letter next to the correct answer or answers to each of the multiple-choice questions below.

1) What is the main topic of the lecture?
   (A) The use of children and animals in psychological experiments
   (B) Psychological research into feelings about food
   (C) Tracing how people develop fear
   (D) The theory of classical conditioning

2) Why does the professor show a picture of a piece of banana cream pie?
   (A) To introduce the topic of conditioning
   (B) To see if his students are paying attention
   (C) To prove that everyone has different preferences
   (D) To explain why classical conditioning always works

3) In Pavlov's experiment, how did the dogs react to hearing a signal?
   (A) They became aggressive.
   (B) Their mouths began to water.
   (C) They learned to fear the signal.
   (D) They walked to the regular feeding place.

4) What did John Watson do in his experiment?
   (A) He proved that children enjoy hearing loud noises.
   (B) He conditioned rats to attack a child.
   (C) He conditioned a child to fear an animal.
   (D) He taught a child to cry when hungry.

5) At the end of the experiment, why did little Albert cry when he saw the rat?
   (A) He thought that the rat did not like him.
   (B) He was frustrated that he could not touch it.
   (C) He wanted to keep the rat as a pet.
   (D) He associated the rat with loud, scary noises.

6) Listen to **Track 3.08**.
   What does the professor suggest when he says this?
   (A) He believes the experiment was harmful to little Albert.
   (B) He thinks Watson was the greatest psychologist in history.
   (C) He does not approve of using rats in experiments.
   (D) He wants to replicate the experiment in class.

Take notes as you listen to the lecture on **Track 3.09**. Then answer the multiple-choice questions that follow.

Art History

Hieronymus Bosch
triptych
The Temptation of Saint Anthony

Things to Consider

WHAT is the lecture about?

WHAT details contribute to the main idea?

WHY does the speaker present the lecture information?

HOW does the speaker organize and present the lecture?

Notes

Circle the letter next to the correct answer or answers to each of the multiple-choice questions below.

1) What is the main subject of the lecture?
   (A) The influence of religion on medieval painting
   (B) A famous painter from the Renaissance period
   (C) Dutch beliefs about the Christian Bible
   (D) How wood has been used in religious art

2) Which of the following are some of Hieronymus Bosch's influences?
   (A) Biblical stories and Dutch proverbs
   (B) Greek mythology and poetry
   (C) Medieval science and medicine
   (D) European nature and American food

3) Listen to **Track 3.10**.
   Why does the professor say this?
   (A) To refute claims made by many art critics
   (B) To explain why Bosch's works are unpopular
   (C) To identify some characteristics of Bosch's art
   (D) To explain why Bosch's works are hard to interpret

4) Listen to **Track 3.11**.
   What can be inferred from this?
   (A) Bosch wanted to depict Saint Anthony as a good, virtuous man.
   (B) Bosch's triptychs were designed to criticize Dutch politicians.
   (C) Bosch was only concerned with becoming wealthy.
   (D) Bosch and Saint Anthony were good friends.

5) Match each description with the correct term.

   Place the letter in front of each description under the heading that it describes.
   Use each description only once.

   (A) The town that Bosch was named after.
   (B) A painting that depicts a man resisting worldly pleasures.
   (C) A work of three paintings on wood panels.

's-Hertogenbosch	Triptych	*The Temptation of Saint Anthony*

Take notes as you listen to the conversation on **Track 3.12**. Then answer the multiple-choice questions that follow.

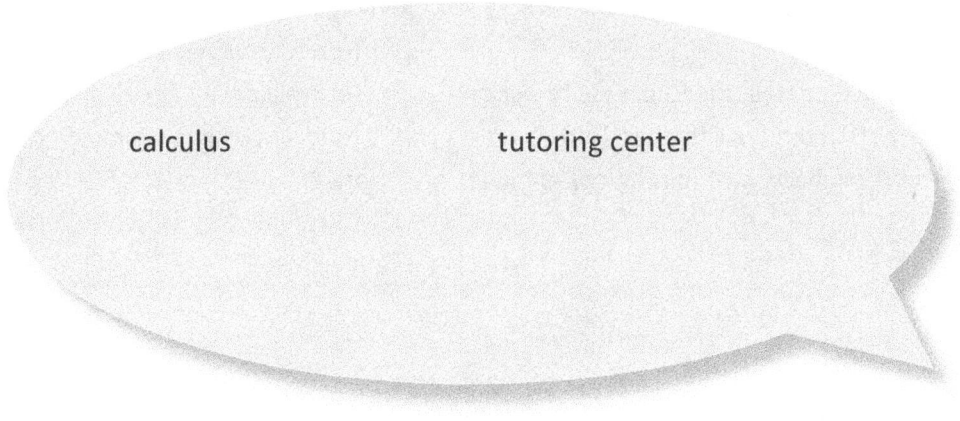

calculus   tutoring center

Things to Consider

WHAT is the conversation about?

WHAT details contribute to the main idea?

WHY are the speakers having the conversation?

HOW do the speakers organize and present the conversation?

Notes

_____
_____
_____
_____
_____
_____
_____
_____
_____

Circle the correct answer or answers to each of the multiple-choice questions below.

1) What subject is the woman studying?
   (A) Writing
   (B) Calculus
   (C) Education
   (D) Tutoring

2) How does the woman feel at the beginning of the conversation?
   (A) Frustrated
   (B) Bored
   (C) Peaceful
   (D) Funny

3) What does the man advise the woman to do?
   (A) Study with him
   (B) Learn to write better
   (C) Talk to her high school teachers
   (D) Go to the tutoring center

4) What can be inferred about the man?
   (A) He never wanted to attend college.
   (B) He learned math from the woman.
   (C) He entered the university early.
   (D) He had difficulty with his classes as a freshman.

5) What will the woman do next?
   (A) Open her book
   (B) Go to the tutoring center
   (C) Do her homework
   (D) Talk to her professor

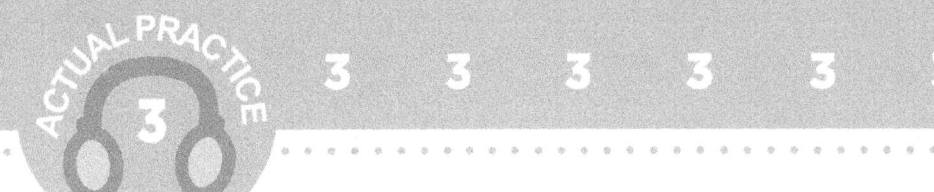

Take notes as you listen to the lecture on **Track 3.13**. Then answer the multiple-choice questions that follow.

Literature

Realism   objectivity
Classicism   *The Jungle*
Romanticism

Things to Consider

WHAT is the lecture about?

WHAT details contribute to the main idea?

WHY does the speaker present the lecture information?

HOW does the speaker organize and present the lecture?

Notes

_____
_____
_____
_____
_____
_____
_____
_____

Circle the letter next to the correct answer or answers to each of the multiple-choice questions below.

1) What is the main topic of the lecture?
   (A) An influential artistic and literary movement
   (B) A famous novel about romantic love
   (C) The similarities between writing and painting
   (D) Why writing about real-life experiences is difficult

2) What does the professor say about Realism at the beginning of the lecture?
   (A) It is no longer used today.
   (B) It is still popular in drama and fiction.
   (C) It is found in classical music.
   (D) It is characterized by romance and emotion.

3) What is the goal of Realism?
   (A) To depict all people as logical and rational
   (B) To make life seem emotionally exciting and satisfying
   (C) To describe life as accurately as possible
   (D) To convince people that life is sad and difficult

4) Listen to **Track 3.14**.
   Why does the professor say this?
   (A) To criticize realist authors
   (B) To explain why Realism developed
   (C) To describe literary movements more popular than Realism
   (D) To refute common beliefs about Realism

5) Which of the following is an example of a Realist theme in literature?
   (A) The search for life's meaning
   (B) The victory of knowledge over ignorance
   (C) The importance of upbringing
   (D) The beauty and innocence of nature

6) Which of the following can be inferred about *The Jungle*, by Upton Sinclair?
   (A) It is a realist work of literature.
   (B) It is a Romantic work of literature.
   (C) It was written before the 1800s.
   (D) It is rarely read by university students.

Take notes as you listen to the lecture on **Track 3.15**. Then answer the multiple-choice questions that follow.

Biology

- contagious yawning
- empathy
- social mammals

Things to Consider

WHAT is the lecture about?

WHAT details contribute to the main idea?

WHY does the speaker present the lecture information?

HOW does the speaker organize and present the lecture?

Notes

_____
_____
_____
_____
_____
_____
_____
_____

Circle the letter next to the correct answer or answers to each of the multiple-choice questions below.

1) What does the professor mainly discuss?
   (A) The benefits of yawning
   (B) The problem with contagious yawning
   (C) The connection between yawning and empathy
   (D) The brain chemicals involved in yawning

2) Listen to **Track 3.16**.
   What does the professor imply when she says this?
   (A) Talking about yawning has made some students yawn.
   (B) The students have become more interested in the lecture.
   (C) The students have started looking at each other.
   (D) Some of the students have fallen asleep.

3) According to the professor, what social mammals experience contagious yawning?
   Choose 2 answers.
   (A) Horses
   (B) Elephants
   (C) Wolves
   (D) Apes

4) Why does the professor mention brain scans?
   (A) To describe the various types of research on yawning
   (B) To explain exactly how empathy developed
   (C) To illustrate the importance of yawning to survival
   (D) To introduce evidence that yawning and empathy are linked

5) Why is communication an advantage for social species?
   (A) They are more likely to sleep at the same time.
   (B) It helped them cooperate on matters of food and territory.
   (C) It helps them keep track of their relationships.
   (D) They will be more willing to defend each other.

6) How does the professor organize the lecture?
   (A) She defines a term and talks about similar terms.
   (B) She explains the causes of a medical condition.
   (C) She describes a phenomenon, and then connects it to a larger research topic.
   (D) She describes various research methods.

Take notes as you listen to the conversation on **Track 3.17**. Then answer the multiple-choice questions that follow.

> museum class trip   offering a ride

Things to Consider

WHAT is the conversation about?

WHAT details contribute to the main idea?

WHY are the speakers having the conversation?

HOW do the speakers organize and present the conversation?

Notes

_____
_____
_____
_____
_____
_____
_____
_____

Circle the letter next to the correct answer or answers to each of the multiple-choice questions below.

1) What is the main topic of the conversation?
   (A) Taking the campus bus to class
   (B) Convincing the man to come on a class trip
   (C) Organizing transportation for a class trip
   (D) Getting directions to a museum

2) Where are the students going for Dr. Tatum's class?
   (A) The Museum of Natural History
   (B) The Museum of Contemporary Art
   (C) The Museum of Ancient Cultures
   (D) The Museum of Aeronautics

3) Why is the man unable to text Alicia?
   (A) He left his phone in his dorm room.
   (B) Alicia does not own a cell phone.
   (C) Alicia's cell phone is turned off.
   (D) He does not have Alicia's phone number.

4) What can be inferred about the relationship between the two speakers?
   (A) They know each other from Dr. Tatum's class.
   (B) They live together in the same dorm building.
   (C) They have never met each other before this conversation.
   (D) They do not share any of the same classes.

5) What will the man probably do after this conversation?
   (A) Get on the bus to go to the museum
   (B) Go to the library to find Alicia
   (C) Go to his upcoming class
   (D) Go for a walk with the woman

Take notes as you listen to the lecture on **Track 3.18**. Then answer the multiple-choice questions that follow.

Microbiology

bacteria
human body
immune system

Things to Consider

WHAT is the lecture about?

WHAT details contribute to the main idea?

WHY does the speaker present the lecture information?

HOW does the speaker organize and present the lecture?

Notes

_____
_____
_____
_____
_____
_____
_____
_____

Circle the letter next to the correct answer or answers to each of the multiple-choice questions below.

1) What is the lecture mainly about?
   (A) The various ways that bacteria harm the body
   (B) The relationship between bacteria and viruses
   (C) A general introduction to bacteria in the human body
   (D) The types of bacteria in our homes and communities

2) Why does the professor mention dangerous, harmful bacteria?
   (A) To explain how to avoid bacteria-related illness
   (B) To contrast them with harmless and beneficial bacteria
   (C) To illustrate the importance of research about bacteria
   (D) To explain how bacteria become dangerous

3) Listen to **Track 3.19**.
   Why might the information just presented "come as a surprise to many"?
   (A) Human bodies contain more bacteria than many people realize.
   (B) Bacteria are much more dangerous than most people realize.
   (C) Most people believe that bacteria cannot survive in humans.
   (D) There are too many types of bacteria to count.

4) What is one result of bacteria being much smaller than human cells?
   (A) The bacteria multiply rapidly.
   (B) Little is known about bacteria.
   (C) Bacteria do not do anything that affects human health.
   (D) Bacteria take up little space in the body.

5) The professor discusses several ways that we acquire bacteria. What can be inferred about the professor's attitude toward acquiring bacteria?
   (A) The processes are natural and ordinary.
   (B) The processes can be changed.
   (C) The processes are rare and mysterious.
   (D) The processes lead to disease.

6) According to the professor, which of the following are ways that some bacteria help us?
   Choose 2 answers.
   (A) They help us get energy from our food.
   (B) They help us find food in our environments.
   (C) They help our immune systems fight harmful bacteria.
   (D) They help us have healthier skin.

Take notes as you listen to the lecture on **Track 3.20**. Then answer the multiple-choice questions that follow.

Things to Consider

WHAT is the lecture about?

WHAT details contribute to the main idea?

WHY does the speaker present the lecture information?

HOW does the speaker organize and present the lecture?

Notes

_____
_____
_____
_____
_____
_____
_____
_____

Circle the letter next to the correct answer or answers to each of the multiple-choice questions below.

1) According to the professor, why is Louis Pasteur significant?
   (A) He invented a way to improve the taste of alcohol.
   (B) He developed many useful antibiotics.
   (C) He contributed to the understanding of alcohol.
   (D) He developed a simple way to prevent many illnesses.

2) Listen to **Track 3.21**.
   What does the professor imply when he says this?
   (A) Pasteur thought that wine was the only liquid that spoiled.
   (B) Pasteur was a well-known scientist even before he developed pasteurization.
   (C) Pasteur was an alcohol manufacturer before he became a scientist.
   (D) Pasteur thought that it was impossible to determine how wine spoils.

3) What does the professor imply about the "tiny organisms" in the spoiled alcohol?
   (A) They are attracted to spoiled alcohol.
   (B) They caused the alcohol to spoil.
   (C) They were not able to survive in liquid.
   (D) They were beneficial to humans.

4) What does the professor's discussion of spontaneous generation illustrate?
   (A) How unhealthy most people's diets used to be
   (B) How common flies and maggots were at the time
   (C) The public's misunderstanding of food and drink spoilage
   (D) The reason that Pasteur became interested in studying wine

5) How is pasteurization different from boiling?
   (A) Pasteurization is not quite as effective as boiling.
   (B) Pasteurization can only be performed on alcohols.
   (C) Pasteurization occurs at a lower heat than boiling.
   (D) Pasteurization requires more equipment than boiling.

6) Listen to **Track 3.22**.
   How does this relate to the lecture as a whole?
   (A) It connects Pasteur's discovery to the present day.
   (B) It proves that pasteurization is effective.
   (C) It explains the dangers of drinking milk and juice.
   (D) It transitions to the topic of dairy foods.

ACTUAL PRACTICE 5

Take notes as you listen to the conversation on **Track 3.23**. Then answer the multiple-choice questions that follow.

> volunteer club
> community service

Things to Consider

WHAT is the conversation about?

WHAT details contribute to the main idea?

WHY are the speakers having the conversation?

HOW do the speakers organize and present the conversation?

Notes

_____
_____
_____
_____
_____
_____
_____
_____

Circle the letter next to the correct answer or answers to each of the multiple-choice questions below.

1) Why does the student go to see the advisor?
   (A) To join a campus club
   (B) To complain about a campus club
   (C) To start a new campus club
   (D) To ask about community needs

2) According to the student, what do many students want to do?
   (A) Help people who are ill
   (B) Help poor and homeless people
   (C) Help more students come to college
   (D) Help improve the quality of campus clubs

3) Listen to **Track 3.24**.
   What does the advisor mean when he says this?
   (A) The student has made a bad proposal.
   (B) The student's idea needs more details.
   (C) The student must come back later and try again.
   (D) The student's idea is not going to work.

4) Why does the student mention recruiting student volunteers?
   (A) She wants students to volunteer to help the advisor.
   (B) She wants to protest a controversial issue.
   (C) She hopes that student volunteers will do all her work.
   (D) She hopes that student volunteers can help community groups.

5) How does the advisor help the student?
   (A) He offers to help the student run her club.
   (B) He signs several forms that the student needs.
   (C) He promises to contact community groups.
   (D) He gives the student some paperwork to fill out.

Take notes as you listen to the lecture on **Track 3.25**. Then answer the multiple-choice questions that follow.

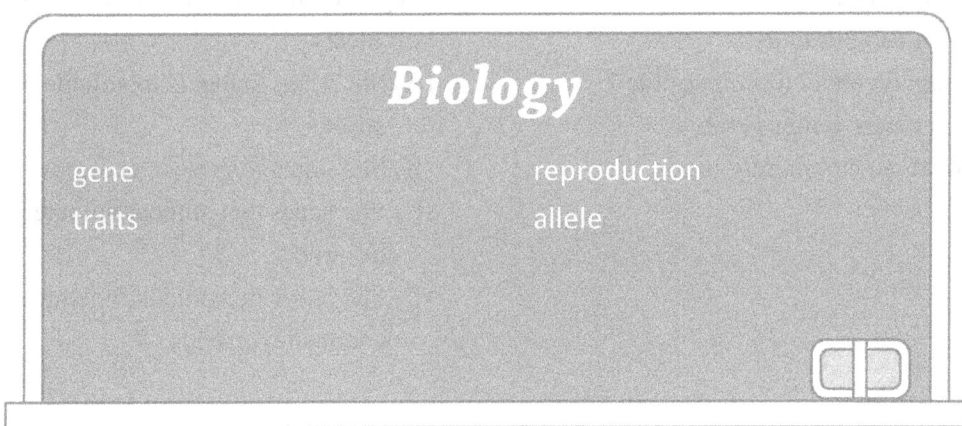

Things to Consider

WHAT is the lecture about?

WHAT details contribute to the main idea?

WHY does the speaker present the lecture information?

HOW does the speaker organize and present the lecture?

Notes
_____
_____
_____
_____
_____
_____
_____
_____

Circle the letter next to the correct answer or answers to each of the multiple-choice questions below.

1) What does the professor mainly discuss?
   (A) How to read a genetic sequence
   (B) What DNA is and how it can affect behavior
   (C) What exactly is meant by the term "alleles"
   (D) What genes are and how they create individuals

2) According to the professor, what are some of the traits that come from genes?
   Choose 2 answers.
   (A) Blood type
   (B) Luck
   (C) Lifespan
   (D) How you look

3) Why does the professor discuss the passing of genes from parent to offspring?
   (A) To explain two types of reproduction
   (B) To explain how DNA affects development
   (C) To explain how life began on Earth
   (D) To explain a famous scientific experiment

4) Listen to **Track 3.26**.
   What does the professor imply when he says this?
   (A) Asexual reproduction is more interesting that sexual reproduction.
   (B) Asexual reproduction tends to occur in simpler life forms.
   (C) Asexual reproduction only occurs among aquatic creatures.
   (D) Asexual reproduction has caused the extinction of many species.

5) Listen to **Track 3.27**.
   Why does the professor say the phrase, "Believe it or not"?
   (A) To explain that he does not believe in genetics
   (B) To show uncertainty about what he is about to say
   (C) To indicate that a surprising fact will follow
   (D) To argue with a student who doubts his claims

6) What is the name for a variation of a gene?
   (A) An allele
   (B) A DNA sequence
   (C) An offspring difference
   (D) A genetic error

Take notes as you listen to the lecture on **Track 3.28**. Then answer the multiple-choice questions that follow.

Chemistry

- atom
- proton
- neutron
- nucleus
- electron
- electric charge

Things to Consider

WHAT is the lecture about?

WHAT details contribute to the main idea?

WHY does the speaker present the lecture information?

HOW does the speaker organize and present the lecture?

Notes

Circle the letter next to the correct answer or answers to each of the multiple-choice questions below.

1) What is the main topic of the lecture?
   (A) The electric charge of electrons
   (B) The structure of an atom
   (C) The atomic weights of different elements
   (D) The formation of subatomic particles

2) According to the professor, which of the following particles form an atom's nucleus?
   Choose 2 answers.
   (A) Protons
   (B) Gluons
   (C) Bosons
   (D) Neutrons

3) Listen to **Track 3.29**.
   Why does the professor say this?
   (A) To transition to the topic of electric charge
   (B) To emphasize that mass is more important than electric charge
   (C) To clarify the relationship between mass and electric charge
   (D) To explain how most electricity is created

4) What is the relationship between the mass of a proton and the mass of an electron?
   (A) Electrons are more massive than protons.
   (B) Protons and electrons have nearly the same masses.
   (C) Protons are more massive than electrons.
   (D) The masses of protons and electrons are unknown.

5) Check the boxes where the description matches the term.

   Check each box in which the term in the left column matches the description of electrical charge in the top row.

	Neutral charge	Positive charge	Negative charge
Proton			
Neutron			
Electron			

Take notes as you listen to the conversation on **Track 3.30**. Then answer the multiple-choice questions that follow.

- final exam
- family vacation

Things to Consider

WHAT is the conversation about?

WHAT details contribute to the main idea?

WHY are the speakers having the conversation?

HOW do the speakers organize and present the conversation?

Notes

_____
_____
_____
_____
_____
_____
_____
_____

Circle the letter next to the correct answer or answers to each of the multiple-choice questions below.

1) Why does the student go to visit the professor?
   (A) To explain why he is not ready to take the final exam
   (B) To retake the final exam
   (C) To see if he can take the final exam today
   (D) To see if he can take the final exam early

2) What does the student ask about the exam?
   (A) To take it home with him on June 5th
   (B) To take it today, because he is leaving on June 5th
   (C) To take it early, on Friday, June 5th
   (D) To see if the professor could postpone it until Friday, June 5th

3) What kind of exam will the professor provide for the student?
   (A) A more difficult test
   (B) An essay exam
   (C) An older version of the test
   (D) A different version of the test

4) Listen to **Track 3.31**.
   Why does the professor say this?
   (A) To show that she does not think that the student cheats
   (B) To joke with the student
   (C) To show that she suspects the student of cheating
   (D) To emphasize the importance of the final exam

5) What will the student probably do immediately after speaking with his professor?
   (A) Speak to his other professors
   (B) Study for the final exam
   (C) Leave for his vacation
   (D) Drop the class

Take notes as you listen to the lecture on **Track 3.32**. Then answer the multiple-choice questions that follow.

Archaeology

Chauvet Cave
cave paintings

Things to Consider

WHAT is the lecture about?

WHAT details contribute to the main idea?

WHY did the speaker present the lecture information?

HOW does the speaker organize and present the lecture?

Notes

_____
_____
_____
_____
_____
_____
_____
_____

Circle the letter next to the correct answer or answers to each of the multiple-choice questions below.

1) What does the professor mainly discuss?
   (A) The discovery of a number of unique cave paintings
   (B) The types of animals that prehistoric people hunted
   (C) How prehistoric cave paintings can be preserved or ruined
   (D) Prehistoric ceremonies that probably involved cave paintings

2) What does the professor imply about the rocks that blocked the entrance of the cave?
   (A) They were easy to remove from the cave's entrance.
   (B) They contained minerals that people were mining.
   (C) They protected the art for 25,000 years.
   (D) They were dangerous during the clearing process.

3) According to the professor, what do the cave paintings depict?
   (A) Dozens of different animal species
   (B) Successful hunting raids
   (C) Symbols of life and death
   (D) People and animals together

4) What does the professor imply about the purpose of the drawings?
   (A) The drawings were meant to scare away intruders.
   (B) Researchers are not sure what purpose the drawings served.
   (C) The drawing showed hunters which animals to attack.
   (D) Researchers believe that the drawings have no purpose.

5) What evidence does the professor offer that the paintings are NOT hunting guides?
   (A) Humans rarely hunted the hyenas, bears, and lions that are depicted.
   (B) Chauvet Cave does not contain prehistoric hunting tools.
   (C) There are no injured animals in the paintings.
   (D) Prehistoric people loved hyenas, bears, and lions.

6) What is the professor going to discuss next?
   (A) Theories about how the artists created the drawings
   (B) The now-extinct animals depicted in the cave
   (C) How the paintings at Chauvet are unique
   (D) Theories about why people made the cave paintings

Actual Test

CHAPTER 4

Actual Test Information

In this section, you will listen to a series of academic lectures and campus-related conversations. After each lecture and conversation, you will answer a series of multiple-choice questions about what you have just heard. Multiple-choice questions are worth one point each, and chart-based, "organizing information" questions are worth two points each.

Because this is the introductory book in *KALLIS' iBT TOEFL Listening* Series, the lectures and conversations here are shorter and simpler than the ones that you will encounter when you take the official iBT TOEFL. Here, each lecture and conversation will last from one to three minutes.

When you take the official iBT TOEFL, you will have 60 to 90 minutes to listen to the lectures and conversations and to answer all the corresponding questions. Because of the reduced lecture and conversation lengths in this book, you should spend no more than 45 minutes completing the Actual Test portion of this book.

	Very Poor	Poor	Good	Very Good	Excellent
Points	1 - 10	11 - 16	17 - 23	24 - 29	30 - 34
Scale	1 - 9	10 - 14	15 - 21	22 - 26	27 - 30

ACTUAL TEST

Take notes as you listen to the lecture on **Track 4.01**. Then answer the multiple-choice questions that follow.

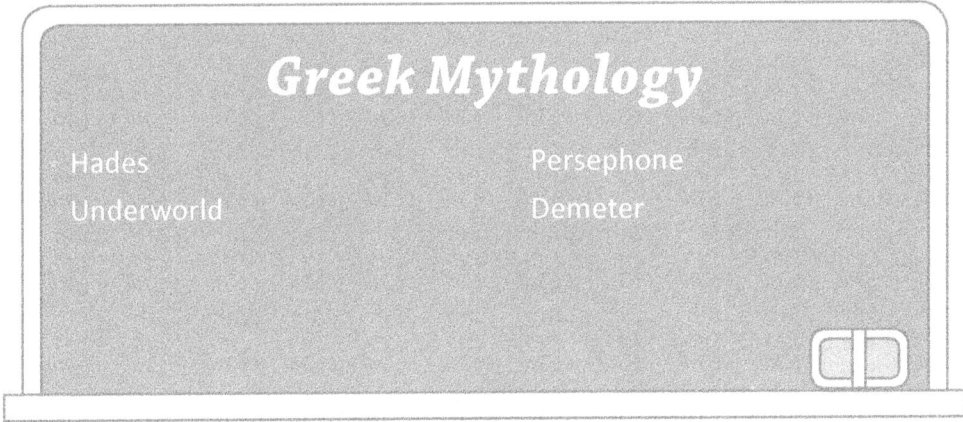

Notes

Listening 1

Circle the letter next to the correct answer or answers to each of the multiple-choice questions below.

1) What is the main topic of the lecture?
   (A) The differences between myths and legends
   (B) A myth that explains why seasons occur
   (C) The marriage customs of ancient civilizations
   (D) A famous story that has influenced many authors

2) What is the name of the Greek god associated with death?
   (A) Persephone
   (B) Hades
   (C) Demeter
   (D) Underworld

3) Listen to **Track 4.02**.
   Why does the professor say this?
   (A) To criticize modern dating practices as "old-fashioned"
   (B) To explain the main difference between ancient and modern cultures
   (C) To emphasize the extremeness of Hades' actions by using humor
   (D) To humorously transition to a new Greek myth

4) Why did Demeter prevent any crops from growing?
   (A) She was upset that Hades took her daughter away.
   (B) She ran out of seeds to plant crops.
   (C) She wanted Hades to love her instead of Persephone.
   (D) She wanted Hades to control the Underworld.

5) According to Greek beliefs, what event caused spring and summer to arrive each year?
   (A) Demeter rewarding humans for their kindness and honesty
   (B) Persephone going to live with her mother, Demeter
   (C) Persephone returning to the Underworld to live with Hades
   (D) Demeter's tears, which fall to the earth as rain

6) What can be inferred about the professor?
   (A) She believes that Persephone, Demeter, and Hades really exist.
   (B) She has never taught a college class before this one.
   (C) She does not enjoy talking about ancient myths.
   (D) She is very knowledgeable about Greek mythology.

ACTUAL TEST 2 2 2 2 2 2 2

Take notes as you listen to the lecture on **Track 4.03**. Then answer the multiple-choice questions that follow.

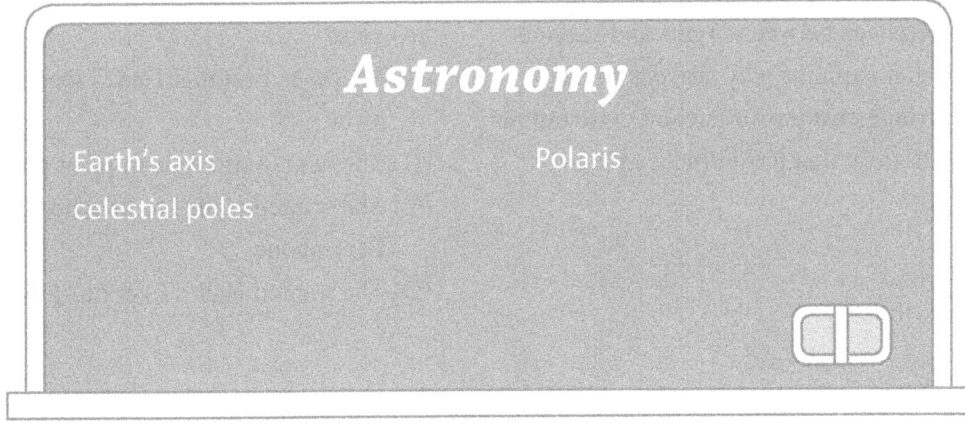

Notes

Listening 2

Circle the letter next to the correct answer or answers to each of the multiple-choice questions below..

1) What is the main topic of the lecture?
   (A) Careers in astronomy
   (B) The difference between planets and moons
   (C) The apparent movement of the stars
   (D) Units of distance used by astronomers

2) Why is the professor holding the lecture outside at night?
   (A) He was locked out of his classroom.
   (B) He wants to show the students the Moon through a telescope.
   (C) He wants to show the students how the Earth rotates.
   (D) He wants students to observe the stars.

3) What causes stars' apparent movement in the sky?
   (A) The Earth's rotation around its own axis.
   (B) The shifting of the north and south poles.
   (C) The changing of clocks by one hour each year.
   (D) The use of telescopes to look at the sky.

4) Which of the following are names that have been given to the star Polaris?

   Click on 2 answers.

   (A) "North Star"
   (B) "Stationary Star"
   (C) "Super Star"
   (D) "Guiding Star"

5) Check the boxes where the description matches the term.

   Check each box where the definition in the left column matches the term in the top row.

	Celestial pole	Western horizon	Eastern horizon
Stars appear to rise here			
Stars appear to descend here			
Stars appear to rotate around this			

ACTUAL TEST 3

Take notes as you listen to the conversation on **Track 4.04**. Then answer the multiple-choice questions that follow.

GRE tests English-literature anthologies
graduate program English-literature subject test

Notes

Listening 3

Circle the letter next to the correct answer or answers to each of the multiple-choice questions below.

1) How many times has the student taken the GRE English-literature subject test?
   (A) Once
   (B) Twice
   (C) Three times
   (D) Four times

2) What subject does the student want to study in graduate school?
   (A) English
   (B) Math
   (C) Science
   (D) Engineering

3) In approximately what percentile did the student score when he took the GRE subject test?
   (A) 10th percentile
   (B) 20th percentile
   (C) 50th percentile
   (D) 80th percentile

4) What will the student try to do to raise his score on the GRE?
   (A) Study with the woman
   (B) Go to the library
   (C) Study math and science
   (D) Read anthologies

5) What will the student probably do next?
   (A) Go to the library
   (B) Retake the GRE
   (C) Read an anthology
   (D) Eat dinner with the woman

ACTUAL TEST 4

Take notes as you listen to the lecture on **Track 4.05**. Then answer the multiple-choice questions that follow.

American History

- Yellowstone region
- Cornelius Hedges
- President Ulysses Grant
- Yellowstone National Park

Notes

Circle the letter next to the correct answer or answers to each of the multiple-choice questions below.

1) What is the main topic of the lecture?
   (A) How Montana became a U.S. territory
   (B) The establishment of Yellowstone National Park
   (C) Why governments must protect the land
   (D) Exploring the western United States

2) What made people want to make Yellowstone into a national park?
   (A) Its strange natural wonders
   (B) Its location near a river
   (C) Its usefulness to the economy
   (D) Its popularity with hunters

3) Listen to **Track 4.06**.
   What does the professor imply about Yellowstone when he says this?
   (A) It was relatively unexplored before the 1800s.
   (B) It is very small region.
   (C) It can only be accessed by boat.
   (D) It is always very hot there.

4) What did Cornelius Hedges do?
   (A) Discourage exploration of the Montana Territory
   (B) Propose that Yellowstone be preserved as a national park
   (C) Decide a court case for the National Park Service
   (D) Build a resort near the Madison River

5) When was Yellowstone National Park established?
   (A) 1850
   (B) 1870
   (C) 1872
   (D) 1892

6) Listen to **Track 4.07**.
   Why does the professor say this?
   (A) To point out the challenges of creating a national park
   (B) To give examples of national parks that are better than Yellowstone
   (C) To emphasize that California is the most beautiful state
   (D) To show how quickly the U.S. National Parks System developed

ACTUAL TEST 5

Take notes as you listen to the conversation on **Track 4.08**. Then answer the multiple-choice questions that follow.

> research paper
> bibliography
> evidence

Notes

Listening 5

Circle the letter next to the correct answer or answers to each of the multiple-choice questions below.

1) Why does the student want to talk to the professor?
   (A) To ask about a grade
   (B) To learn about an author
   (C) To get help with typing
   (D) To receive some writing tips

2) Listen to **Track 4.09**.
   What can be inferred from this?
   A) The student does not understand the professor's grading system.
   B) The student feels that she deserved a better grade.
   C) The student is very happy with the grade she received.
   D) The student believes that she completed the wrong assignment.

3) What has the woman failed to include in her assignment?
   (A) quotes
   (B) paragraphs
   (C) a bibliography
   (D) a grade

4) What is the main problem with the assignment?
   (A) It is written and not typed.
   (B) It was copied from another person.
   (C) It was turned in one month late.
   (D) It does not have enough evidence.

5) What does the professor advise the student to do?
   (A) Talk with him before the next assignment
   (B) Get her information from a different book
   (C) Use fewer words to explain herself
   (D) Stop complaining about her problems

ACTUAL TEST 6

Take notes as you listen to the lecture on **Track 4.10**. Then answer the multiple-choice questions that follow.

American History

- branches of government
- Executive
- Legislative
- Judicial
- British monarchy

Notes

Listening 6

Circle the letter next to the correct answer or answers to each of the multiple-choice questions below.

1) What is the main topic of the lecture?
   (A) The differences between U.S. and British governments
   (B) The successes of recent U.S. presidents
   (C) The structure of the U.S. government
   (D) The benefits of being ruled by a monarchy

2) Which of the following are branches of the U.S. government?
   Click on 2 answers.
   (A) The Legal Branch
   (B) The American Branch
   (C) The Judicial Branch
   (D) The Legislative Branch

3) Who is the head of the Executive Branch of the U.S. government?
   (A) The Supreme Court
   (B) Congress
   (C) The king
   (D) The U.S. President

4) Why does the professor mention the British monarchy?
   (A) To contrast it with the structure of the U.S. government
   (B) To explain its origins and history
   (C) To praise its simplicity and effectiveness
   (D) To criticize its unnecessary complexity

5) Listen to **Track 4.11**.
   What does the professor imply when he says this?
   (A) They appreciated the structure of the British government.
   (B) They included a large number of skilled politicians.
   (C) They did not want one person to have all governmental power.
   (D) They regretted making the U.S. government so complicated.

6) Why does the U.S. government consist of three branches?
   (A) To ensure that there are always government jobs available
   (B) To ensure that none of them become too powerful
   (C) To protect U.S. citizens from the British monarchy
   (D) To protect government officials from angry citizens

APPENDIX

Listening Scripts

CHAPTER 1

TRACK 1.01

Narrator: Listen to a conversation between a student and his professor.

Female Professor (FP): Hi, Sam. How can I help you?

Male Student (MS): Well, you wrote a comment on my research paper saying that I could rewrite it for a better grade, and I was hoping you could give me some advice for rewriting it.

FP: Certainly, I'm glad you asked. Now refresh my memory: what topic did you choose for your paper?

MS: I wrote about how the people of ancient Athens were able to develop a successful democracy.

FP: Ah, that's right. An excellent topic. And if I remember correctly, you made a lot of excellent points in your paper, but none of these points were supported with sufficient evidence. You must back up your claims with evidence, or at least include the opinions of other scholars.

MS: Thanks, professor. I'll be sure to do that.

Narrator: Now get ready to answer the questions.

TRACK 1.02

Narrator: Listen to a conversation between a student and an advisor.

Female Advisor (FA): What can I help you with?

Male Student (MS): Well, I'm a freshman this year. And even though it's only a few weeks into school, I can already tell that I'm going to need more money to pay for supplies and textbooks.

FA: Ah, so you've come to see if there are any jobs available.

MS: Yes, that's why I'm here.

FA: Well, unfortunately, all the most popular on-campus jobs are already taken. But there are still several dining hall positions left.

MS: I'll take anything I can get.

FA: (*Laughs*) That's a good attitude when looking for a job. Here's an application. Just fill this out, give it back to me, and I'll send it to the university's employment office.

MS: Thanks, I'll do that.

Narrator: Now get ready to answer the questions.

TRACK 1.03

Narrator: Listen to a conversation between a student and her professor.

Female Student (FS): Hey, professor. I really enjoyed your lecture on blues music today, but I have a question about something you didn't discuss. I've always associated the harmonica with the United States. Was it invented here?

Male Professor (MP): Well, harmonicas are strongly associated with 19th-century America—American heroes like Wyatt Earp played them on the range, and President Lincoln was said to carry one with him at all times. But the harmonica was actually invented in Europe.

FS: Really?

MP: Absolutely. Prototypes of the harmonica were sold in Austria and Germany in the early 1800s, and an American called Richter improved on these early models. But it was actually a German clockmaker who manufactured the version of the harmonica that became so popular among Americans.

FS: Wow, that's pretty surprising.

MP: I was surprised when I learned that, too.

Narrator: Now get ready to answer the questions.

TRACK 1.04

Narrator: Listen to a conversation between a student and her professor.

Male Professor (MP): Hello, Lisa.

Female Student (FS): Hi, Professor Dunn. So I was wondering if you think I should take your upper-division biology class next year.

MP: Ah, my advanced genetics class. That's a tough class, but you seem to be doing quite well in my lower-division class this quarter. Have you taken organic chemistry yet?

FS: Not yet. That's why I'm wondering if taking your genetics class would be a good idea.

MP: Well, I'd argue that an understanding of organic chemistry is necessary for genetics. I strongly encourage you to take organic chemistry first.

FS: Okay, that makes sense.

Narrator: Now get ready to answer the questions.

TRACK 1.05

Narrator: Listen to a conversation between a student and a university employee.

Male University Employee (ME): How can I help you today?

Female Student (FS): I'm interested in becoming a resident assistant, and I was wondering what I have to do to apply.

ME: Well, you came to the right place. For starters, here's an application for you to fill out. Once we have this information from you, we will look at your academic records, and if all that information looks good, we will call you for an interview.

FS: Awesome! This sounds like a pretty simple process.

ME: We try to make it easy for students to apply for these positions.

Narrator: Now get ready to answer the questions.

TRACK 1.06

Narrator: Listen to a conversation between a student and his professor.

Male Student (MS): Professor, I have a quick question about something related to today's lecture on dance and culture. Have you noticed that dances first considered "shocking" by the general public often become considered "traditional" over time?

Female Professor (FP): Yeah, I'd say that's pretty accurate. Why do you ask?

MS: Well, I was watching this conservative religious program, and they were teaching people how to do the waltz, the tango, and the cha-cha for exercise—you know, as part of this whole ballroom dance craze.

FP: Uh-huh.

MS: And as I watched the program, I thought to myself, 'One hundred years ago, some churches might have been condemning these dances instead of encouraging them.'

FP: That's an interesting observation.

Narrator: Now get ready to answer the questions.

TRACK 1.07

Narrator: Listen to a conversation between a student and a university employee.

Male Student (MS): Hello. May I ask you a few questions?

Female University Employee (FE): Of course. What can I help you with?

MS: Well, I received a letter in my campus mailbox saying that someone filed a noise complaint against me. But I don't really know what that means. Am I in big trouble or something?

FE: Ah, I see. You're not in big trouble. Noise complaints are pretty common. It just means you were playing loud music or something after 10 pm. Just try not to let it happen again. If you get three noise complaints in a year, you have to leave the dorms.

MS: Oh, okay. I will definitely try to keep it down, then. Thanks for your help.

Narrator: Now get ready to answer the questions.

TRACK 1.08

Narrator: Listen to a conversation between a student and his professor.

Male Student (MS): Excuse me, professor. I have a quick question about today's lecture.

Female Professor (FP): How can I help you?

MS: Well, I'm kind of confused about the origins of Romantic literature from the 18th and 19th centuries.

FP: Ah, I see. So today in class, I was making the argument that Romantic literature really stresses the vastness and mystery of nature.

MS: Right, I remember that.

FP: And how was that different from the European scientific revolution that came before it?

MS: Um, didn't the scientific revolution basically say that everything about nature can be classified and understood?

FP: Exactly! So Romantic literature wanted to reintroduce the idea that nature is vast and unknowable.

Narrator: Now get ready to answer the questions.

TRACK 1.09

Narrator: Listen to a conversation between a student and an advisor.

Male Advisor (MA): Good afternoon. What can I do for you?

Female Student (FS): Hi. Well, I'm new to the university, and I was wondering if you could tell me the difference between loans, grants, and scholarships. They all sound like the same thing to me.

MA: I'd be happy to. So a loan is money that either the state or the federal government gives to the student. But you have to pay back the money eventually, with interest.

FS: Okay. But what about grants and scholarships.

MA: The state and federal government provide grants. They go to U.S. citizens who need financial aid to attend college. And you actually don't need to pay back grants. And scholarships are usually given to students for their academic or extracurricular accomplishments. Scholarships don't have to be paid back, either.

FS: Okay, I think I understand now. Thanks!

Narrator: Now get ready to answer the questions.

TRACK 1.10

Narrator: Listen to a conversation between a student and an advisor.

Female Student (FS): Hello. I'm thinking of transferring to a different university, and I was wondering what the downsides of transferring are.

Male Advisor (MA): Okay. For starters, where are you thinking of transferring to?

FS: Well, I looked at a few local universities, including Coast University and United University, but I think I want to transfer to Upstate University because they have the robotics program I'm interested in.

MA: I see. Well, Upstate University has different general education requirements. So unfortunately, you will have to retake some of your general education classes. What is your current major?

FS: Now it's electrical engineering.

MA: That's good. Many electrical engineering classes overlap with robotics, so I think you'll only have to retake your general education classes.

FS: Oh, okay. Thanks for the information.

Narrator: Now get ready to answer the questions.

TRACK 1.11

Narrator: Listen to a conversation between a student and her professor.

Male Professor (MP): Hello, Dinah. It's good to see you coming to my office hours.

Female Student (FS): Thanks, professor. I'm actually coming in because I missed the first ten minutes of class, so I wanted to know what you lectured about in that time.

MP: Certainly, I'm glad you asked. So do you remember what we discussed last week?

FS: Yeah, last week you talked about the formation of our solar system.

MP: That's right. And because so many students missed that lecture, I just reviewed some major points regarding the formation of the solar system.

FS: Oh, awesome. So you just went over stuff I should already know.

MP: (*Laughs*) That's right.

Narrator: Now get ready to answer the questions.

TRACK 1.12

Narrator: Why does the student say this?

FS: Oh, awesome. So we just went over stuff I should already know.

TRACK 1.13

Narrator: Listen to a conversation between a student and a librarian.

Female Student (FS): Excuse me. Can I ask you a question?

Male Librarian (ML): Certainly. How can I help you?

FS: Well, it's my first time in the library, and I was wondering if you could point out where the books on engineering are.

ML: You'll have a hard time finding those. You're in the wrong library.

FS: What do you mean? I thought this was the main campus library.

ML: It is. But all the engineering books are in the Science and Engineering Library, located about a 10-minute walk east of here.

FS: I see. No wonder I couldn't find any science books here. Well, thanks for your help.

Narrator: Now get ready to answer the questions.

TRACK 1.14

Narrator: Listen to part of the conversation, and then answer the question.

FS: Well, it's my first time in the library, and I was wondering if you could point out where the books on engineering are.

Narrator: Why does the student say this?

FS: Well, it's my first time in the library…

TRACK 1.15

Narrator: Listen to a conversation between a student and her professor.

Female Student (FS): Excuse me, professor. I was wondering if you had any book recommendations. Anthropology and mythology seem really interesting, and I'm looking for a book that covers pretty basic concepts.

Male Professor (MP): Of course I can recommend some reading. Let's see…. Have you heard of the 19th-century anthropologist named James Frazer?

FS: I haven't.

MP: I see. Well, his book, *The Golden Bough*, is a bit dated, but it was among the first books to try to point out the common roots of all the world's religions. Very ambitious stuff for the 1800s.

FS: That sounds great. Thanks very much for the recommendation, professor.

MP: My pleasure. Let me know what you think of the book.

Narrator: Now get ready to answer the questions.

TRACK 1.16

Narrator: Listen to part of the conversation, and then answer the question.

FS: Excuse me, professor. I was wondering if you had any book recommendations. Anthropology and mythology seem really interesting, and I'm looking for a book that covers pretty basic concepts.

Narrator: Why does the student say this?

FS: …I'm looking for a book that covers pretty basic concepts.

TRACK 1.17

Narrator: Listen to a conversation between a student and a librarian.

Male Student (MS): I'd like to return these library books, please.

Female Librarian (FL): Of course. Just hand me the books and your student ID, please.

(*Student gives the books and his ID to the Librarian*)

FL: It appears as though these books are each two weeks overdue.

MS: No way! I thought students could check out books for one month at a time.

FL: I'm afraid not. That was our policy a few years ago, but currently, students can only check out books for two weeks at a time.

MS: I see. Well, I guess I'll pay the late fees now, then.

Narrator: Now get ready to answer the questions.

TRACK 1.18

Narrator: Why does the student say this?

MS: No way! I thought students could check out books for one month at a time.

TRACK 1.19

Narrator: Listen to a conversation between a student and her professor.

Female Student (FS): Professor, I've been around a lot of collies and poodles, so I know they're smart dogs. But I was wondering, are there studies that have measured the intelligence of different types of dogs?

Male Professor (MP): Well, there's a great book on the topic by a researcher in Canada. In the book, he measures the ability of each dog breed to "obey a first command" as his standard for intelligence.

FS: So if the dogs obeyed a command quickly, they were deemed "intelligent" by the researcher?

MP: Exactly.

FS: So, how did collies and poodles do on the researcher's tests?

MP: They ranked numbers one and two respectively, just as you thought.

Narrator: Now get ready to answer the questions.

TRACK 1.20

Narrator: Listen to part of the conversation, and then answer the question.

FS: Professor, I've been around a lot of collies and poodles, so I know they're smart dogs. But I was wondering, are there studies that have measured the intelligence of different types of dogs?

Narrator: Why does the student say this?

FS: Professor, I've been around a lot of collies and poodles, so I know they're smart dogs.

TRACK 1.21

Narrator: Listen to a conversation between a student and an advisor.

Female Advisor (FA): What can I help you with, sir?

Male Student (MS): I'm a freshman this year, and I'm thinking of doing a double major, but I'm not sure I can finish both majors in four years.

FA: Okay. What are the two majors that you're interested in?

MS: Well, I know it sounds kind of strange, but I want to major in physics and history.

FA: Well, from start to finish, the physics major consists of 19 classes, and the history major consists of 14 classes. So with your general education classes, you'd have to take over 40 classes in four years.

MS: Is that too many?

FA: If you're willing to take a couple of extra classes each year, it's possible, but it will definitely be difficult.

MS: Huh. I'll have to weigh my options. Thanks for your help.

Narrator: Now get ready to answer the questions.

TRACK 1.22

Narrator: What can be inferred from this statement?

MS: Well, I know it sounds kind of strange, but I want to major in physics and history.

TRACK 1.23

Narrator: Listen to a conversation between a student and his professor.

Male Student (MS): Professor, I know your office hours are over, but I wanted to ask you a quick question: has anyone ever studied the phenomenon of people singing in the bathroom?

Female Professor (FP): Not that I know of, Josh, but that's an interesting topic.

MS: I know. I often find myself singing in the shower. I like how the shower tiles make my voice echo and give it a fuller, deeper sound.

FP: That's a good observation. You know, many famous musicians have noted the same thing.

MS: Really?

FP: Uh-huh. Paul Simon, of the folk duo *Simon and Garfunkel*, said that he wrote the song "The Sounds of Silence" in a darkened bathroom due to these effects.

MS: Wow.

Narrator: Now get ready to answer the questions.

TRACK 1.24

Narrator: Listen to a conversation between a student and her professor.

Female Student (FS): Excuse me, professor. Can I ask you a few questions.

Male Professor (MP): Certainly. What can I do for you?

FS: I was wondering if you can tell me what kind of stuff you're going to include in the final exam.

MP: Well, even I'm not *exactly* sure what will be on the exam yet (*Laughs*), but I guess I can give you some information now. You'll have to translate two or three of the passages that we have studied this quarter, and you will have to tell me what parts of speech certain words from the passage are.

FS: Oh, the test doesn't sound nearly as hard as I thought it would. Thanks for the heads up!

Narrator: Now get ready to answer the questions.

TRACK 1.25

Narrator: Which word best describes the student's tone in this part of the conversation?

FS: Oh, the test doesn't sound nearly as hard as I thought it would. Thanks for the heads up!

TRACK 1.26

Narrator: What does the professor suggest when he says this?

MP: Well, even I'm not exactly sure what will be on the exam yet.

TRACK 1.27

Narrator: Listen to a conversation between a student and his professor.

Female Professor (FP): Hi, Liam. What can I help you with?

Male Student (MS): Well, I'm working on the water pollution project that you assigned.

FP: Ah, yes. Have you collected water samples from five local water sources?

MS: I have. And I've even run the recommended tests on them. (*Sounding frustrated*) But my results were much different than what I had predicted. So now I don't know what to write in my conclusion.

FP: That's okay. In your conclusion, you can talk about the differences between what you expected to find and what you actually found. You can suggest some possible reasons for these differences, too.

MS: Oh, really? I didn't realize I could do that. Thanks, professor. I think you just saved my project!

Narrator: Now get ready to answer the questions.

TRACK 1.28

Narrator: Which word best describes the student's tone in this part of the conversation?

MS: But my results were way different than what I had predicted. So now I don't know what to write in my conclusion.

TRACK 1.29

Narrator: Listen to a conversation between a student and an advisor.

Male Advisor (MA): Hi there. What can I help you with?

Female Student (FS): Hi. I want to switch majors, but I don't really know what I need to do to get that done.

MA: Well, luckily for you, switching majors is a pretty easy process. So what's your current major?

FS: Sociology.

MA: Okay, so you're studying sociology now. And what major do you want to switch to?

FS: Evolutionary biology.

MA: Interesting. Okay, here's the form to switch majors. First, you need to have the head of the biology department sign on these two lines. Once that's done, come back to me and I'll walk you through the rest of the process.

FS: Sounds good. I'll come back with that signature in a little while.

Narrator: Now get ready to answer the questions.

TRACK 1.30

Narrator: Listen to a conversation between a student and a university employee.

Female Student (FS): Excuse me, sir. Do you work here?

Male University Employee (ME): Yes, in the textbook section of the store.

FS: Great. I'm taking a class called Music Theory 160. There's supposed to be a book of sheet music that goes with the textbook, but I don't see it on the shelf.

ME: Let me just check our computer. (*University employee types the book's information into computer*) It looks like we just sold the last one this morning.

FS: Oh, darn. What am I supposed to do now?

ME: Well, they've already been reordered. We should have new ones in by next week.

FS: But my class starts tomorrow.

ME: Hmm. I'm a classical music buff, so I happen to know that the book your professor is using is fairly popular.

FS: Oh, so you have a copy I can borrow?

ME: No, but I have seen it at the record store down the street. It's less than a mile from the university.

FS: I'll try there. Thanks for your help.

Narrator: Now get ready to answer the questions.

TRACK 1.31

Narrator: Listen to a conversation between a man and an advisor.

Female Advisor (FA): Hello. How can I help you?

Male Speaker (MS): I want to apply to your university as an undergraduate. Can I pick up an application here?

FA: No, this is the Financial Aid Office. You need to go to the Registrar's Office. Do you know where the library is?

MS: Um, not really. This is my first time on campus.

FA: Well, let me show you on a map. We're here, at the southern end of the campus. The library is about one-hundred yards north of here.

MS: So I can just walk straight through that grove of eucalyptus trees to get there?

FA: Exactly. The Registrar's is the building to the right of the library. I'll circle the Registrar's on the map for you.

MS: Thanks.

FA: Oh, while you're here, you might as well pick up a financial aid packet. You might be eligible for assistance.

MS: Great. Considering the tuition rates at this school, I'll need it.

Narrator: Now get ready to answer the questions.

TRACK 1.32

Narrator: Listen to part of the conversation, and then answer the question.

FA: Oh, while you're here, you might as well pick up a financial aid packet. You might be eligible for assistance.

MS: Great. Considering the tuition rates at this school, I'll need it.

Narrator: What does the man imply about the university when he says this?

MS: Great. Considering the tuition rates at this school, I'll need it.

TRACK 1.33

Narrator: Listen to a conversation between a student and a university employee.

Male Student (MS): I lost my student ID the other day, so I need a replacement.

Female University Employee (FE): Well, you've come to the right place for that. First, I need to see some other form of picture ID, like a driver's license or a passport. That way I can confirm that, you know, I'm printing an ID for the right person.

MS: Oh, okay. I'll have to go get my driver's license from my dorm room. I didn't think I'd need it.

FE: Sounds good. And while you're there, you might want to grab your wallet because it costs 15 dollars to print a new student ID.

MS: You're kidding! It's just a little piece of plastic!

FE: Well, I guess the school needs some way to discourage students from losing their IDs all the time.

MS: I guess I've learned my lesson. Well, I'll be back with my license and 15 dollars in a few minutes.

FE: Okay, see you soon.

Narrator: Now get ready to answer the questions.

TRACK 1.34

Narrator: Listen to part of the conversation, and then answer the question.

FE: Sounds good. And while you're there, you might want to grab your wallet because it costs 15 dollars to print a new student ID.

MS: You're kidding! It's just a little piece of plastic!

Narrator: Why does the student say this?

MS: You're kidding! It's just a little piece of plastic!

TRACK 1.35

Narrator: Listen to a conversation between a student and her professor.

Male Professor (MP): Hey, Lucia. What can I help you with?

Female Student (FS): Well I'm thinking of applying to one of the lab internships offered over the summer.

MP: Oh, I'm glad to hear that. Those summer internships can be really helpful for gaining practical lab experience.

FS: Yes, that's exactly what I've heard. But I've also heard that the internships are pretty hard to get because there's so much competition, so I was wondering if you could write me a letter of recommendation.

MP: Okay, sure. I'd be happy to. You've always turned in excellent work, so I'll gladly write you a recommendation. Do you know what project the lab will be working on this year?

FS: I think the professor is researching something about the relationship between matter and the energy it releases.

MP: Ah, sounds like spectroscopy. That should be interesting. Well, let me see. Today is Thursday, so I'll have the letter of recommendation ready by Monday.

FS: Great! Thank you so much, professor!

Narrator: Now get ready to answer the questions.

TRACK 1.36

Narrator: Listen to a conversation between a student and a university employee.

Male Student (MS): Hello. I was hoping you could help me with something. I can't seem to get on the Internet in my dorm room.

Female University Employee (FE): Hmmmm, that's strange. Do you know if anyone in your dorm has Internet access?

MS: When I asked others in my building, they said they couldn't access the Internet either. And I've tried restarting my computer and reconnecting to the Internet, but I really don't know what else to do.

FE: I don't think there's much more you can do. I'll have to send one of our repair people to check on the school's wireless Internet system.

MS: Do you think the Internet will be working soon? I have to finish a report.

FE: I'm sorry, but I really can't say. It depends on what kind of problem the repair person finds. But you can always study in the library. It's always quiet there, so you can focus on writing your report, and the Internet is working fine there.

MS: Okay, I'll do that.

FE: And we'll send an email to everyone in your dorm building when the problem is solved.

MS: Sounds great. Thanks!

Narrator: Now get ready to answer the questions.

TRACK 1.37

Narrator: Listen to part of the conversation, and then answer the question.

MS: Do you think the Internet will be working soon? I have

to finish a report.
Narrator: Why does the student say this?
MS: I have to finish a report.

CHAPTER 2

TRACK 2.01

Narrator: Listen to part of a lecture in a contemporary art class.
Female Professor (FP): So really, any drawn or written messages that are painted, or more often spray-painted, onto public spaces without permission are considered graffiti. Now some people consider graffiti an art form. This view has become more and more popular over the past few decades because many "street artists" have begun spray-painting images
and designs that not only look good, but also convey some sort of political or social message. On the other hand, many people, police officers included, consider graffiti to be an act of vandalism. So let's get a discussion going here—is graffiti art, or is it vandalism?
Narrator: Now get ready to answer the questions.

TRACK 2.02

Narrator: Listen to part of a lecture in a psychology class.
Female Professor (FP): Depression affects between 7 and 10 percent of Americans. Now a lot of people think that being depressed means getting sad for no reason. But sadness is a passing emotion that
everyone feels at one point or another, while depression affects every part of a person's life. And whereas the cause of temporary sadness is usually easy to identify, there's no one, easily treatable cause of depression. Traumatic events, drug abuse, and even a person's genes can increase a person's chance of experiencing depression.
Narrator: Now get ready to answer the questions.

TRACK 2.03

Narrator: Listen to part of a lecture in an ancient history class.
Male Professor (MP): Today, I'd like to get into the origins of the flag. One of the first types of fabric flag recognized by historians is called the *vexillum*, which was carried by Roman cavalry. If you've ever seen any Hollywood movies about ancient Rome, you've seen models of *vexillum*. The *vexillum* was a square piece of cloth hung on a bar at the end of a spear. This flag served as a meeting place for ancient Roman soldiers in battle. And it must have been a successful strategy, because Europeans derived their flags from the *vexillum* and carried them in a similar manner until the Middle Ages.
Narrator: Now get ready to answer the questions.

TRACK 2.04

Narrator: Listen to part of a lecture in an ancient history class.
Female Professor (FP): You may have heard that salt was worth its weight in gold in ancient times. Although this claim may be an exaggeration, salt was once much more valuable than it is today. This is because salt was the best preservative around in the days before refrigeration. In fact, salt was so valuable in some regions that it was used as a commodity. For example, our modern word "salary" comes from the Latin word *salarium*, which translates to "salt
money." *Salarium* originally referred to the amount of salt paid to Roman soldiers for their services.
Narrator: Now get ready to answer the questions.

TRACK 2.05

Narrator: Listen to part of a lecture in a mechanical engineering class.
Male Professor (MP): Of all the common types of engine, the diesel engine is the most efficient. It can produce the greatest amount of mechanical energy using the smallest amount of fuel. The diesel engine is so efficient because of the way it mixes air and fuel to create energy. Now you may be wondering, 'What's so special about mixing air and fuel?' Well, it has to do with how much the air gets compressed; in other words, how much pressure the air gets put under. And as the air compresses, it heats up, so when a little fuel is added to the compression chamber, it combusts because of the heated air. This resulting explosion provides the energy that runs the engine.
Narrator: Now get ready to answer the questions.

TRACK 2.06

Narrator: Listen to part of a lecture in a philosophy class.

Male Professor (MP): So now I'd like to make an interesting point about the word "philosophy." Just a couple centuries ago, many of the subjects now taught in European and American schools were all part of a very broad field called "philosophy." Physics, chemistry, biology, astronomy, government, mathematics, ethics, and even music were all considered proper subjects for attention by philosophers. As recently as the early 19th century, "natural philosopher" was a term for a student of any of the sciences, so all you biology and chemistry majors out there would have been natural philosophers a couple hundred years ago. And specialists in ethics were called "moral philosophers."

Narrator: Now get ready to answer the questions.

TRACK 2.07

Narrator: Listen to part of a lecture in an American history class.

Female Professor (FP): So the American state of Georgia plays a big role in the economy of the southeastern part of the United States. Atlanta, which is Georgia's capital and the state's largest city, is the commercial, transportation, and financial center of the entire southeastern U.S. Consequently, thousands of national businesses have offices in Atlanta. Although many people think of Georgia as a state of small towns and rural areas, urban manufacturing centers are more representative of the state today.

Narrator: Now get ready to answer the questions.

TRACK 2.08

Narrator: Listen to part of a lecture in a musicology class.

Male Professor (MP): Today I'd like to talk about the banjo, an instrument that is very much a part of American folk music. The banjo is a long-necked instrument with a body shaped like a small round drum. Its five strings are plucked like a guitar and make a distinctive, rough sound when played. The banjo probably made its way to America during the slave trade, where it became associated with the culture of Southern blacks. During its early history, the banjo went by many names, such as "bangie," "banza," and "banger." In fact, in the late 18th century, President Thomas Jefferson called the instrument a "banjar" when he remarked on the impressive skills of black banjo players.

Narrator: Now get ready to answer the questions.

TRACK 2.09

Narrator: Listen to part of a lecture in an ecology class.

Male Professor (MP): When most people think of a wasp, they imagine an aggressive, flying insect with a sharp, painful sting. But in reality, wasps can be quite helpful to humans, especially farmers. For example, some species of wasp prey on insects that are harmful to crops, namely caterpillars. And, just like bees, many species of wasp feed on nectar, which helps with pollination as the wasps travel from one flower to another. And, in spite of their reputation, wasps only sting humans when threatened or provoked.

Narrator: Now get ready to answer the questions.

TRACK 2.10

Narrator: Listen to part of a lecture in a sociology class.

Female Professor (FP): In the United States, there are two basic ways that the federal government has tried to help poor people with housing. The first way is for the government to build and operate public apartment buildings, where it can charge low rents based on the family's income. The federal government built a lot of public housing projects in the 1950s and 1960s. But over time, many of the projects turned into areas filled with poverty, racial segregation, and crime. Now, the federal government prefers to help poor people by giving them "vouchers" to help pay rent for private apartments. Vouchers may help people move to neighborhoods where there are more opportunities, especially for jobs.

Narrator: Now get ready to answer the questions.

TRACK 2.11

Narrator: Listen to part of a lecture in a marine biology class.

Male Professor (MP): Although all the marine sponges we have looked at so far look quite similar, there are marine sponges of many different shapes and sizes. For example, some sponges are flat, like the ones seen in the slides, but others are tall, tree-shaped structures with branching tubes. Pretty strange looking, huh? And while some sponges are relatively small, others can grow up to two meters tall. Most marine sponges you see at aquariums and on television are textured and soft, but there are many species that are smooth and hard, like rocks. Let's take a look at some of this variety right now, shall we?

Narrator: Now get ready to answer the questions.

TRACK 2.12

Narrator: Listen to part of a lecture in a physiology class.

Female Professor (FP): Most people drink coffee because it contains a drug called "caffeine," which stimulates the central nervous system. An ordinary cup of coffee contains about 150 milligrams of caffeine—roughly the amount that physicians regard as a "therapeutic dose". Once consumed, caffeine tends to give people more energy and focus. To a limited degree, it
shortens reaction time and improves efficiency in well-learned motor tasks, such as typing. When
consumed in the evening, coffee causes sleeplessness in some people, but others don't have trouble getting to sleep after drinking coffee.

Narrator: Now get ready to answer the questions.

TRACK 2.13

Narrator: Why does the professor say this?

FP: When consumed in the evening, coffee causes sleeplessness in some people…

TRACK 2.14

Narrator: Listen to part of a lecture in a biology class.

Female Professor (FP): Let me just repeat what I've said about the physical differences between African and Asian elephant species. On its front feet, the African elephant has four toenails while the Asian elephant has five. Also, African elephants have much larger ears than Asian elephants. Finally, while virtually all African males and most females have tusks, many Asian males and nearly all females are tuskless. And though these physical differences seem minor, African and Asian elephants are unable to interbreed because they are too genetically different. In fact, the only crossbred elephant baby died shortly after its birth.

Narrator: Now get ready to answer the questions.

TRACK 2.15

Narrator: Listen to part of a lecture in an American history class.

Male Professor (MP): Since today is the first day of daylight savings, I want to give you some historical background on this annual time switch. Believe it or not, the idea of setting clocks ahead to have more day-time during waking hours was first suggested in 1784 by America's own Benjamin Franklin,. But it wasn't until World Wars I and II that some countries, including the United States, adopted the idea of a summer daylight savings time. But even then, not every state participated in daylight savings time until the Uniform Time Act of 1966. And I can tell you from first-hand experience, traveling from one state to another and not knowing what time it was before the Time Act made for some interesting experiences.

Narrator: Now get ready to answer the questions.

TRACK 2.16

Narrator: Why does the professor say this?

MP: And I can tell you from first-hand experience, traveling from one state to another and not knowing what time it was before the Time Act made for some interesting experiences.

TRACK 2.17

Narrator: Listen to part of a lecture in an architecture class.

Male Professor (MP): In my opinion, the architecture of ancient Greek theaters is simply amazing. First of all, the Greek theaters are huge structures that are open to the air. In many of these theaters, up to twenty thousand people could sit on the blocks built in a terraced circle around the acting space, which is called the "orchestra." The theaters were built into hillsides to support the terraced seating. Greek theaters also have excellent acoustics, which were designed to carry the actors' voices to the entire
audience. In one theater, which still stands today, a pin dropped in the orchestra can be heard even from the furthest seat.

Narrator: Now get ready to answer the questions.

TRACK 2.18

Narrator: Why does the professor say this?

MP: In one theater, which still stands today, a pin dropped in the orchestra can be heard in the farthest seat.

TRACK 2.19

Narrator: Listen to part of a lecture in an ancient history class.

Female Professor (FP): Cats may have been domesticated 10,000 years ago, at about the same time and in the same places that humans started growing wheat and barley. Cats probably became domesticated because they were very effective at catching the mice and rats that would have eaten grain harvests. There were even cat gods and goddesses in the religions of ancient China, India, and Egypt. Later, Islamic culture revered cats for protecting books from mice. But ancient Greeks had an unusual attitude about cats because Greeks commonly had pet ferrets to catch mice. In Greek myth, the cat assisted the moon goddess, who lived in the world of the dead.

Narrator: Now get ready to answer the questions.

TRACK 2.20

Narrator: Listen to part of a lecture in a literature class.

Male Professor (MP): Today, we begin our unit on myths. Now the word "myth" is often mistakenly understood to mean "fiction"—that is, something that never happened. But in truth, myths are just a way of thinking about the past. A famous historian, Mircea Eliade, once put it this way: "Myths tell only of that which really happened." So by this, Eliade doesn't mean to suggest that myths correctly explain what actually occurred in the past. What she means—and I'm fully with her on this account—is that myths provide greatly altered accounts of real events. Let me illustrate this principle right now with Homer's famous epic, the *Iliad*.

Narrator: Now get ready to answer the questions.

TRACK 2.21

Narrator: Listen to part of the lecture, and then answer the question.

MP: What she means—and I'm fully with her on this account—is that myths provide greatly altered accounts of real events.

Narrator: What does the professor mean when he says this?

MP: ...and I'm fully with her on this account.

TRACK 2.22

Narrator: Listen to part of a lecture in an American literature class.

Female Professor (FP): During the 17th and 18th centuries, most American literature came from the Northern colonies and states. Much of the early literature from the Northern colonies was religious in nature. But most Southern colonists were more focused on farming than writing about their religious experiences. Also, Southern farms tended to be isolated in the countryside, so children had few opportunities for education. In the Northern colonies, many people lived in cities, which tend to be more fruitful for literary production. But despite this early drought, the South overflowed with "fruit" of its own during the 19th and 20th centuries.

Narrator: Now get ready to answer the questions.

TRACK 2.23

Narrator: What does the author imply about the South when he says this?

FP: But despite this early drought, the South overflowed with "fruit" of its own during the 19th and 20th centuries.

TRACK 2.24

Narrator: Listen to part of a lecture in a paleontology class.

Male Professor (MP): One of the many questions that paleontologists wonder about is whether dinosaurs could see color. Well, the closest relatives to dinosaurs that are around today are birds, and birds can distinguish colors. But then again, birds evolved under different conditions than dinosaurs, so maybe birds needed to distinguish colors whereas dinosaurs did not. What paleontologists do know for certain is that nearly all dinosaur skulls have large eye sockets and large optic lobes, shown by the imprint left on the fossil bones that surrounded their brains. Therefore, dinosaurs were probably very birdlike in being visually oriented. However, there's still heated debate over the topic of dinosaur vision.

Narrator: Now get ready to answer the questions.

TRACK 2.25

Narrator: What does the professor mean when he says this?

MP: However, there's still heated debate over the topic of dinosaur vision.

TRACK 2.26

Narrator: Listen to part of a lecture in a chemistry class.

Female Professor (FS): Let's talk about plastic, a material that most of us come into contact with every day of our lives. There are over 50 types of plastic, and new types are being developed as scientists continue to research this versatile material. Different plastics are used for different purposes, but most of them tend to be strong, lightweight, and resistant to decay. They are often less expensive to produce than other materials and can be made in a wide variety of colors.

Narrator: Now get ready to answer the questions.

TRACK 2.27

Narrator: What does the professor imply when she says this?

FP: …new types are being developed as scientists continue to research this versatile material.

TRACK 2.28

Narrator: Listen to part of a lecture in a nutritional sciences class.

Male Professor (MP): So now that we've looked at some of the science behind fats, proteins, carbohydrates, and fibers, I want to begin talking about vitamins, which are some of the other essential components of nutrition. Now can anyone tell me what a vitamin is?

Female Student (FS): Isn't a vitamin a kind of substance that the body needs a little bit of to function properly?

MP: More or less, yeah. But I'd like to add to your description a bit. A "vitamin" is a substance that an organism doesn't produce naturally, so it needs to get that compound from its environment. So because different plants and animals naturally produce different compounds, the compounds that are considered vitamins vary from organism to organism. For example, most animals and pretty much all plants produces vitamin C naturally. So, for most creatures, vitamin C isn't really a vitamin, it's a naturally produced acid. But primates lost the ability to produce vitamin C millions of years ago. So primates, including humans, must eat food with vitamin C in it to survive. Because we have to consume it, vitamin C is, well, a vitamin to humans. Now let's see *why* vitamins are so necessary by looking at the role of vitamin C in the human body.

Narrator: Now get ready to answer the questions.

TRACK 2.29

Narrator: Listen to part of the lecture, and then answer the question.

FS: Isn't a vitamin a kind of substance that the body needs a little bit of to function properly?

MP: More or less, yeah.

Narrator: Why does the professor say this in response to the student's answer?

MP: More or less, yeah.

TRACK 2.30

Narrator: Listen to part of a lecture in an economics class.

Female Professor (FP): Adam Smith was a Scottish philosopher who has been called the father of modern economics. In 1776, Smith published *The Wealth of Nations*, which still influences discussions about buying and selling goods in society.

Adam Smith said that for an economy to be efficient, each person must be free to seek his or her own financial success. So, imagine that a shoemaker bargains with a customer and sells a pair of shoes at the highest price that he can. Then the shoemaker goes to a farmer's market and bargains for the lowest possible prices for food. Smith said that such bargaining is a form of cooperation among people. It results in an efficient way of meeting everyone's needs. In my simple example, farmers will get shoes, and shoemakers will get farm goods. So by meeting one's own needs, one is contributing to the public good. Smith said that in free and fair markets, people are "led by an invisible hand" to do what is best for everyone.

Some people say that Smith believed that the government should not interfere at all. But actually, he said the opposite. He said that what ruins a market's efficiency is when a few people conspire to raise prices. One example would be if all the shoemakers in a town get together and set high prices for shoes. The so-called "invisible hand" would be thrown off. In Smith's view, the government must watch the marketplaces carefully in order to break up such groups and keep everything fair.

Narrator: Now get ready to answer the questions.

TRACK 2.31

Narrator: Why does the professor say this?

FP: Some people say that Smith believed that the government should not interfere at all. But actually, he said the opposite.

TRACK 2.32

Narrator: Listen to part of a lecture in a physics class.

Male Professor (MP): Welcome to Physics 1A. Before we start memorizing equations and conducting experiments, I want to cover some basics. In everyday speech, people often use the terms "mass" and "weight" as if they have the same meaning. But really, these terms are not interchangeable. In the world of physics, these words have completely different meanings.

I'll start with mass. Every object has "mass," which is the amount of matter that something contains. So anything you can touch consists of matter, and therefore it has mass.

"Weight" is a measurement of how much gravity is pulling on an object. So if I flew away from Earth in a spaceship, my weight would decrease as I flew further away from Earth's gravitational pull. Eventually, I'd weigh as little as the surrounding air in my spaceship, and I'd be able to float around freely. But even in outer space, far away from Earth's gravity, my body would still contain the same amount of matter as it did on Earth, so my mass in outer space is equal to my mass on Earth.

Narrator: Now get ready to answer the questions.

TRACK 2.33

Narrator: Listen to part of the lecture, and then answer the following question.

MP: So anything you can touch consists of matter, and therefore it has mass.

Narrator: Why does the professor mention "anything you can touch"?

TRACK 2.34

Narrator: Listen to part of a lecture in a psychology class.

Female Professor (FP): Now I'd like to briefly cover a phenomenon known as "phantom limb syndrome." As you know, the word "phantom" means "ghost." But the phantoms we'll discuss today relate to science more than superstition. Many people who must have limbs surgically removed, most commonly arms, legs, and fingers, report experiencing sensations where the missing limb would normally be. Essentially, these people feel like the missing part of the body is still attached; we call this "phantom limb syndrome." And phantom limb syndrome is much more common than you might think: up to 80 percent of amputee patients report having phantom limb sensations.

Now this becomes a real medical concern when people report feeling pain in the limb, even though the limb is no longer attached to the body. How can a doctor treat such pain? Unfortunately, researchers have come up with some interesting hypotheses, but not with a definite answer. The cause of this really troubling syndrome remains a mystery. So let's open this up for discussion. Based on what you have learned so far about the brain, which areas of the brain might possibly be responsible for this sensation? Where would you start your research?

Narrator: Now get ready to answer the questions.

TRACK 2.35

Narrator: Why does the professor say this?

FP: As you know, the word "phantom" means "ghost." But the phantoms we'll discuss today relate to science more than superstition.

TRACK 2.36

Narrator: Listen to part of a lecture in an American history class.

Female Professor (FP): In 1867, the United States' Secretary of State William Seward negotiated the Alaska Purchase with Russia. As the name suggests, the "Alaska Purchase" refers to the U.S. buying the territory that's now the state of Alaska from Russia. And even though the U.S. bought this giant piece of land cheaply, for just 7.2 million dollars, some

Americans were upset about the deal. You see, Seward negotiated the purchase right after the U.S. Civil War, and Americans thought that the U.S. government needed to spend its money on rebuilding its war-torn communities. But these critics soon silenced themselves. It wasn't long before the U.S. began to make huge amounts of money from Alaska. In the late 1800s, gold was found in the Alaska territory. And today, the state exports a huge amount of petroleum.

Male Student (MS): But why did Russia give up such a huge piece of land for such a low price?

FP: Ah, well, in the 1800s, Russia and Britain were enemies, and Canada still belonged to the British. Russia wanted to sell Alaska because Russian rulers worried that they would not be able to defend the territory from British Canada. At the same time, Russia thought that surrounding British Canada by American territories would help control British power.

Narrator: Now get ready to answer the questions.

CHAPTER 3

TRACK 3.01

Narrator: Listen to part of a lecture in a design class.

Male Professor (MP): So in the early 20th century, we can see modernist designs in art that rejected fancy Victorian decorations and details. Instead, modernist design aimed for very simple forms that could be mass-produced in factories. The emphasis was on being affordable and useful to ordinary people.

One source of many modernist designs was a special trade school in Germany called Bauhaus, which was open from 1919 to 1933. In its workshops, the Bauhaus school tried to bring together fine arts, such as painting and sculpture, with consumer products. For example, the Bauhaus school created wallpaper designs that included big, bold geometric shapes and colors. With this wallpaper, there would be no need to hang any pictures on the wall. As a result, people could decorate with industrial products, in this case wallpaper, that were mass-produced in a factory rather than having to buy expensive hand-painted and framed art for decoration.

The Bauhaus school had an especially important influence on the design of simple furniture. For example, one of the Bauhaus instructors, Marcel Breuer, is famous for creating an armchair inspired by a bicycle. The story is that, in 1925, Breuer took a look at his bicycle and reasoned that bent metal tubes could just as easily form a chair as they could a bicycle. So, he created a bent steel armchair frame with strips of canvas across the seat, the back, and the arms. Some may consider it less attractive and comfortable than a stuffed armchair, but it was certainly inexpensive to produce in a factory. Now let's talk about some of the other modernist design schools whose designs were influenced by the Bauhaus.

Narrator: Now get ready to answer the questions.

TRACK 3.02

Narrator: What can be inferred about modernist designers from this?

MP: For example, one of the Bauhaus instructors, Marcel Breuer, is famous for creating an armchair inspired by a bicycle. The story is that, in 1925, Breuer took a look at his bicycle and reasoned that bent metal tubes could just as easily form a chair as they could a bicycle.

TRACK 3.03

Narrator: Listen to a conversation between a student and a *Daily Tribune* employee.

Female Employee (FE): Hello, this is the *Daily Tribune Newspaper*'s publishing office. How may I help you?

Male Student (MS): Hello. My name is Brad Williams. I'm calling about your advertisement in the university career center. It says you have an internship available.

FE: Yes, we are accepting applications for it now. You realize this is a volunteer position, right? Interns receive university class credit, but no salary.

MS: Oh, I'm aware of that. I just want to get some experience working at a real newspaper. I'm hoping to become a journalist after I graduate.

FE: That's great. Are you majoring in journalism at the moment?

MS: No, in English. But I write a weekly column for the school newspaper.

FE: I see. Well, your next step is to talk to Dr. Henry. He runs the internship program at the university. You can fill out an application form with him.

MS: That sounds easy enough.

FE: And I'd also like to interview you. Do you have time to come into the *Daily Tribune*'s office around four o'clock this afternoon?

MS: Yes, I do.

FE: Great. Oh, and make sure to bring a couple samples of your writing. I'd love to see them.

Narrator: Now get ready to answer the questions.

TRACK 3.04

Narrator: Listen to part of a lecture in a history class.

Female Professor (FP): If you look in my hand, you'll see a fascinating little tool—yes, it's a button. Even in prehistoric times, people made buttons out of bones, shells, or wood. But prehistoric people appear to have used buttons only for decoration. To fasten and secure their clothing, they seem to have used belts and pins. Gradually, buttons became functional rather than just decorative. For example, in 13th-century Europe, wealthy people began using buttons to fasten clothing. Buttons allowed those who could afford it to wear fashions that were pulled tightly from shoulder to hip. The buttons were small spheres that held fabric together by being pushed through loops located on the opposite side of the piece of clothing. Soon the reinforced buttonhole was invented, so loops were no longer necessary.

Until the Industrial Revolution, buttons had to be made by hand, often out of precious metals. But during the mid-1800s, factories began producing flat metal buttons with the four holes in the center. That is the shape we now consider to be "normal," right? The less expensive buttons allowed more men and women to wear the tight-fitting fashions of the 1800s. Men wore button-up vests, and women wore dresses that fit tightly around the waist.

Narrator: Now get ready to answer the questions.

TRACK 3.05

Narrator: Listen to part of a lecture in a music composition class.

Female Professor (FP): So what you just heard was an example of a fugue. As I said before, a fugue is a type of composition in which one instrument starts by playing a melody, called a "subject." After the subject, another instrument enters playing an "answer" to the subject. The answer copies the subject. This pattern continues as more instruments enter the composition.

Male Student (MS): Professor, I think I heard three instruments in this piece. Is that correct?

FP: Yes, it is. Can you tell me which instrument played the subject melody?

MS: I'm pretty sure it was a violin.

FP: That's right. And which instrument played the first "answer" melody?

MS: The flute. But there was something different about the melody the flute played. It wasn't exactly the same; it sounded funny.

FP: Very observant. What you heard was the melody repeated in a different musical key. So the musical pattern was the same, but it was played a fifth higher.

MS: Oh, so that's what it was.

FP: Who can tell me which instrument played the last answer melody?

Female Student (FS): Wasn't it a cello?

FP: Excellent. The cello repeated the subject again in another different musical key.

FS: I noticed something else, professor. After the subject melody was answered by the two other melodies, everything changed.

FP: Yes, it did. We've just described the first part of a fugue called the "exposition." In the second part, there are "developmental episodes" based on the subject and answers in the exposition. We'll talk about that in just a little while.

Narrator: Now get ready to answer the questions.

TRACK 3.06

Narrator: Listen to a conversation between two students.

Female Student (FS): What's wrong, Michael? You look like you're about to cry?

Male Student (MS): Did you get your report card yet?

FS: Yeah, straight "Bs" again. I just can't seem to crack that "A" mark.

MS: Well, get this: I got an "F" in Professor Keller's chemistry class.

FS: An "F"? But that's impossible. You got "As" on every test and project. In fact, if it weren't for you, I probably would've gotten an "F" myself.

MS: I know. It just doesn't make any sense.

FS: Did you talk to Professor Keller about it?

MS: No, he was a visiting professor from Germany, remember? He went back home over winter break.

FS: Oh, right. Well, he obviously made a mistake with your grade. There must be some way to fix it.

MS: But how?

FS: I'd start by going to the chemistry department and getting Professor Keller's phone number in Germany. Then, you can call and explain the situation to him.

MS: I guess you're right. Will you walk over there with me?

FS: Sure, I was going in that direction anyway to meet a friend at the university café.

Narrator: Now get ready to answer the questions.

TRACK 3.07

Narrator: Listen to part of a lecture in a psychology class.

Male Professor (MP): Today's topic is classical conditioning. Now, let's look at a picture here of a piece of banana cream pie. Those of you who love banana cream pie might find your mouths watering. But those of you who hate banana cream pie might feel a little sick. What's going on here? Well, psychologists say that our past experiences *condition* our responses. Any experience of having eaten something like banana cream pie has shaped how we feel about this picture.

Now you have probably heard about Pavlov's dogs. More than 100 years ago, Ivan Pavlov found that if he rang a bell or gave some other signal each time dogs were about to get fed, eventually the dogs' mouths would water when they heard the signal, even if there was no food present. The dogs now had an automatic response. Pavlov said the dogs had been *conditioned* to think about food when they heard the signal.

Later, psychologist John B. Watson conditioned an 8-month-old baby called "little Albert." At first, little Albert seemed to enjoy seeing a laboratory rat. But Watson began to make a loud, frightening noise each time Albert reached out to touch the rat. Soon, every time Albert even caught sight of the rat, he began to cry. He associated the rat with the frightening noise, even when the frightening noise wasn't there. He had been *conditioned* to fear rats. Today such an experiment would be considered unethical because of how poor little Albert was treated, but ultimately, the experiment does demonstrate the effectiveness of classical conditioning.

Narrator: Now get ready to answer the questions.

TRACK 3.08

Narrator: Why does the professor say this?

MP: Today such an experiment would be considered unethical because of how poor little Albert was treated, but ultimately, the experiment does demonstrate the effectiveness of classical conditioning.

TRACK 3.09

Narrator: Listen to part of a lecture in an art history class.

Male Professor (MP): Now let's continue our examination of the "Dutch Masters" from the Renaissance period.

Hieronymus Bosch was a unique Dutch painter who lived during the 15th century. Bosch's name is a variation of 's-Hertogenbosch, the name of the town in the Netherlands where Bosch was born. He's best known for his imaginative triptychs. Triptychs consist of three related paintings that are mounted on wood panels and attached to one another. Bosch's paintings are filled with malformed people, distorted animals, and surreal landscapes. Bosch was influenced by a variety of sources, including Dutch proverbs, Biblical stories, and astrology.

Now let's take a close look at one of Bosch's most famous triptychs, *The Temptation of Saint Anthony*, which was painted in the early 1500s. So as you can see, there's a lot going on in this triptych, but I want you guys to focus on the central panel. Here, we can see Saint Anthony kneeling and facing a small statue of Jesus Christ. It's also important to notice how Anthony turns his back on the malformed people and creatures around him, all of whom are pursuing all these temptations, or activities that make the body feel good, but that corrupt the soul. So this painting is really emphasizing Anthony's ability to turn away from and reject all this corruption and greed that surrounds him.

So you'll notice many weird-looking creatures and people in this triptych. And I'd like to hear your guys' thoughts: what do you guys think some of these figures represent?

Narrator: Now get ready to answer the questions.

TRACK 3.10

Narrator: Why does the professor say this?
MP: Bosch's paintings are filled with malformed people, distorted animals, and surreal landscapes.

TRACK 3.11

Narrator: What can be inferred from this?
MP: It's also important to notice how Anthony turns his back on the malformed people and creatures around him, all of whom are pursuing all these temptations, or activities that make the body feel good, but that corrupt the soul. So this painting is really emphasizing Anthony's ability to turn away from and reject all this corruption and greed that surrounds him.

TRACK 3.12

Narrator: Listen to a conversation between two students.
Female Student (FS): These calculus problems just don't make any sense to me.
Male Student (MS): Yeah, these problems are hard to explain. I don't really know how to put it into words.
FS: Thanks for trying, but I just don't know what to do. I need to pass this class for my general education requirement, but calculus is just impossible for me.
MS: Maybe you should try the university tutoring center.
FS: Tutoring? No way. All my math tutors in high school just ended up making me more confused.
MS: But the tutors at the university have been trained to teach their particular subjects, so they can probably give you shortcuts that will help you grasp calculus.
FS: Do you really think so?
MS: Sure. Remember how bad I was at writing my freshman year?
FS: Oh, yeah. You thought you might have to drop out of the university because of your grades.
MS: I sure did. But the writing tutors taught me a simple essay-writing technique that still gets me "As" to this day.
FS: Wow, that's encouraging.
MS: I know. That's why I think you should give it a try. Why don't we go over there together right now?
FS: Sure, sounds like a good idea.
Narrator: Now get ready to answer the questions.

TRACK 3.13

Narrator: Listen to part of a lecture in a literature class.
Female Professor (FP): We're about to start our unit on Realism. Realism is so widespread in today's fiction and drama that it's no longer recognized as a distinct artistic movement. But this wasn't the case when it started over two hundred years ago.

In literature, Realism describes the attempt to portray life as it is. A Realist author's main goal is to describe, as accurately as possible, what's perceived through the senses.

Realism became the dominant art form in the mid-1800s. At this time, Realism started out as a revolt against Classicism and Romanticism—movements that idealized life. The works of Classicists show life as being more rational and structured than it really is, and Romanticists' works show life as being more emotionally exciting than it normally is.

Realist authors try to be as objective as possible. For instance, Realist authors try to depict things as they really are by leaving their own desires out of their writing. However, in the process of presenting their material, Realist authors cannot help being influenced by what they feel and think. Therefore, even the finest examples of Realist literature are the results of personal judgments.

Common Realist themes today include the importance of upbringing, the oppression of minorities, and the search for values in a hostile world. You'll see all of these illustrated in the first novel we'll read for this unit, Upton Sinclair's *The Jungle*.
Narrator: Now get ready to answer the questions.

TRACK 3.14

Narrator: Why does the professor say this?
FP: At this time, Realism started out as a revolt against Classicism and Romanticism—movements that idealized life.

TRACK 3.15

Narrator: Listen to part of a lecture in a biology class.
Female Professor (FP): Yawning is often associated with sleepiness or boredom, but it can happen for other reasons. You've probably all heard the phrase "yawning is contagious." And it's true that seeing other people yawn, and even talking about yawning or reading about it, can make us want to yawn as well. Ah, I see that some of you are already affected by this discussion!

And the same contagious yawning has been observed among other species, including some apes, wolves, and dogs. And that leads us to our focus question for today: "Why do we yawn when we see others yawn?"

Well, a lot of researchers think that "contagious yawning" has something to do with empathy, which is the ability to relate to another's experiences. In fact, brain scans have shown that yawning activates the same area of the brain as empathy and social knowledge. And on top of that, all those yawning animals I listed a minute ago are social mammals. They have to cooperate with others of the species to find food and defend territory, so being able to communicate with each other is an advantage. So, to tie this in to our earlier discussion, some researchers who study the biology and social psychology of contagious smiling, laughing, and so on, also look at yawning. Understanding contagious yawning may someday provide another clue about how empathy developed in social mammals, including humans.

Narrator: Now get ready to answer the questions.

TRACK 3.16

Narrator: Listen to part of the lecture, and then answer the question.

FP: And it's true that seeing other people yawn, and even talking about yawning or reading about it, can make us want to yawn as well. Ah, I see that some of you are already affected by this discussion!

Narrator: What does the professor imply when he says this?

FP: Ah, I see that some of you are already affected by this discussion!

TRACK 3.17

Narrator: Listen to a conversation between two students.

Female Student (FS): Hey, Matt. Are you going to the Museum of Contemporary Art for Dr. Tatum's class this Saturday?

Male Student (MS): Well, I want to go, but I don't have a ride to the museum, and it takes an hour to get there by bus.

FS: Oh, perfect! I was just about to ask if you wanted a ride. I was hoping to get a group of people from class together to go. Exploring the museum in a group would be more fun than going alone.

MS: Yeah, that'd be great! Thanks for offering a ride.

FS: I'm glad you can come. So far, there are three of us going in my car, so I've got room for you and one more person. Do you know of anyone else who still needs a ride to the museum?

MS: Actually, I think I do. Alicia might still need a ride.

FS: Oh, perfect. Can you text her and ask if she wants to come?

MS: I don't have her phone number, but I'll see her in class in a few minutes. I'll ask her then. Speaking of which, I've got to go to class.

FS: Sounds good. I'll talk to you later, then.

Narrator: Now get ready to answer the questions.

TRACK 3.18

Narrator: Listen to part of a lecture in a microbiology class.

Female Professor (FP): Many people think of bacteria as dangerous, harmful invaders of the human body. After all, bacteria are responsible for outbreaks of deadly illness such as E. coli, cholera, and salmonella. So it may come as a surprise to many to learn that, in the human body, bacteria outnumber human cells at a ratio that could be as high as 10 to 1. Foreign bacteria live and reproduce on our skin, in our mouths, and especially in our intestines. But because bacteria are much smaller than human cells, the trillions of bacteria don't take up too much space in our bodies.

So now you might be asking yourself, "How did all these bacteria get into our bodies?" Well, the bacteria start to arrive right after birth. Lots of bacteria are transferred to an infant during breastfeeding. But even as you grow, you acquire new types of bacteria from the food you eat and the water you drink. (*To student*) Yes, you have a question?

Male Student (MS): So what do all these bacteria do once they're inside our bodies?

FP: Excellent question. Surprisingly, many of them do quite a bit to help us. Some of the bacteria in our intestines help us get more energy from our food. Others help the immune system by fighting off harmful bacteria that people sometimes consume.

Narrator: Now get ready to answer the questions.

TRACK 3.19

Narrator: Listen to part of the lecture, and then answer the question.

FP: So it may come as a surprise to many to learn that, in the human body, bacteria outnumber human cells at a ratio that could be as high as 10 to 1.

Narrator: Why might the information just presented "come as a surprise to many"?

TRACK 3.20

Narrator: Listen to part of a lecture in a history of science class.

Male Professor (MP): Today I want to talk a little bit about chemist and biologist Louis Pasteur, whose research on how to make food and drinks safer has prevented countless illnesses over the past 150 years. Until the 1800s, people weren't exactly sure what caused their food and drink to spoil. So, in 1856, an alcohol manufacturer approached scientist Louis Pasteur and asked him to figure out why some batches of wine spoiled more quickly than others.

So Pasteur used a microscope to compare samples of spoiled alcohol to samples of unspoiled alcohol. When Pasteur did this, he saw that tiny organisms were present only in the spoiled alcohol. These organisms, and really anything that can cause sickness or disease, are called *pathogens*. After a number of experiments, Pasteur determined that the pathogens came from the surrounding environment. Although this idea—that food and beverages get contaminated by things around them—seems like common sense to us today, most people in Pasteur's time believed in spontaneous generation. In other words, when people saw maggots grow on rotting food, they thought the maggots were born from the food itself, not from a fly that laid eggs on it.

Pasteur proposed killing pathogens by heating the liquid. Since boiling the wine would ruin it, he determined the lowest temperature and the least amount of time that wine must be heated at to kill pathogens before sealing the wine in bottles. Although he wasn't the first to suggest all this, Pasteur was the first person to conduct such careful research on the subject. He named this heating process after himself, calling it pasteurization. Today, milk, juices, and many other products are usually pasteurized.

Narrator: Now get ready to answer the questions.

TRACK 3.21

Narrator: What does the professor imply when he says this?

MP: So, in 1856, an alcohol manufacturer approached scientist Louis Pasteur and asked him to figure out why some batches of wine spoiled more quickly than others.

TRACK 3.22

Narrator: How does this relate to the lecture as a whole?

MP: Today, milk, juices, and many other products are usually pasteurized.

TRACK 3.23

Narrator: Listen to a conversation between a student and an advisor.

Male Advisor (MA): Hey, Victoria. What can I do for you?

Female Student (FS): Well, I want to learn about the process of starting a campus club. It seems like a lot of students here would like to get more involved in the community, but they don't know what to do.

MA: That's interesting. Why do you think that?

FS: Well, I was talking to some other people in my sociology class, and they were saying that they want to do more to help out poor families and homeless people. We could not only help others, but also get some practical experience to build on what we learn in class.

MA: Hmmm, that sounds like a good idea, but it's not very specific.

FS: Well, if we have a club, then we can approach community groups and find out what their needs are. Then we can recruit students to volunteer some of their time to meet those needs. We would, you know, introduce volunteers to community groups.

MA: That sounds like a great idea. But before you start planning any projects, you need to get the club approved by the university. Here's the paperwork you need to apply for club status on campus.

FS: Thanks! I'll get started on this now.

Narrator: Now get ready to answer the questions.

TRACK 3.24

Narrator: What does the advisor mean when she says this?

MA: Hmmm, that sounds like a good idea, but it's not very specific.

TRACK 3.25

Narrator: Listen to part of a lecture in a biology class.

Male Professor (MP): So before we get into any of the really complicated stuff, I want to address a very important question: "What is a gene?"

A basic description of a gene is (*slowly*) a segment of DNA that holds information that tells an organism how to grow and develop. In other words, genes determine how you look, your blood type, whether you'll have allergies , and, to a certain extent, your behaviors.

So now that we know what genes are, let's talk about where they come from. For every organism that has ever lived, genes get passed on from a parent to its offspring. In sexual reproduction—where two organisms create offspring—each parent contributes an equal number of genes to its offspring. Thus, you have the same number of genes from your mother as you do from your father. In asexual reproduction—where one organism produces offspring by itself—all offspring are clones of the parent, so they have the exact same genes as their parent. Along with single-celled organisms, some plants, insects, and aquatic organisms such as sea stars reproduce asexually, so their offspring will have the exact same genes as the parent.

Now that we've covered a few of the basics, let's talk about genes in humans. Believe it or not, you share over 99 percent of the exact same genes with every other person in the world. So all the characteristics that make you unique come from less than 1 percent of your genes. These genes' DNA sequences differ slightly from person to person, and these slightly differing genes are called alleles. One example of an allele is the gene that determines eye color. Some people have the allele for blue eyes, others the allele for brown eyes.

Narrator: Now get ready to answer the questions.

TRACK 3.26

Narrator: What does the author imply when he says this?

MP: Along with single-celled organisms, some plants, insects, and aquatic organisms such as sea stars reproduce asexually...

TRACK 3.27

Narrator: Listen to part of the lecture, and then answer the following question.

MP: Believe it or not, you share over 99 percent of the exact same genes with every other person in the world.

Narrator: Why does the professor say the phrase, "Believe it or not"?

TRACK 3.28

Narrator: Listen to part of a lecture in a chemistry class.

Male Professor (MP): Welcome to Chemistry 1. I want to start today's lecture by reviewing some basics. So let's start with the structure of atoms, which combine with each other to form elements, molecules, and all the matter in the universe. Now these tiny atoms are made up of three particles called protons, neutrons, and electrons. The protons and neutrons, which have nearly the same masses, are grouped together at the center of the atom, forming the nucleus of the atom. And the electrons, which have much, much less mass than protons and neutrons, travel around the nucleus.

So like I said, the electron has a lot less mass than the proton and neutron, but it makes up for its small size with an important quality called "electric charge." The electron has a negative electric charge of 1. And though it's much bigger than the electron, the proton has an electric charge that's the exact opposite of the electron—so the proton has a positive electric charge of 1. The neutron, however, is electrically neutral, so it has an electric charge that's neither positive nor negative—that is, an electric charge of 0.

So let's recap. An atom is made of three types of particles: protons, neutrons, and electrons. Positively charged protons and neutrally charged neutrons have nearly the same masses, and they are grouped together to form the nucleus of the atom, which is located at the center of the atom. Negatively charged electrons, which are much smaller than protons or neutrons, travel around the nucleus.

Narrator: Now get ready to answer the questions.

TRACK 3.29

Narrator: Why does the professor say this?

MP: So like I said, the electron has a lot less mass than the proton and neutron, but it makes up for its small size with an important quality called "electric charge."

TRACK 3.30

Narrator: Listen to a conversation between a student and a professor.

Male Student (MS): Hi, professor. Do you have a minute?

Female Professor (FP): Of course, Michael. What can I do for you?

MS: Well, the final exam for your class is on June 8th, right?

FP: That's right

MS: Well, I found out yesterday that my family and I are leaving for a vacation on June 6th, so I won't be here the day of the test.

FP: Ah, so you're wondering if you can take the exam early?

MS: Yeah, is there any way I can take the test the Friday before, so on, ah, June 5th?

FP: Sure, that's fine. But I'll have to give you a different version of the test than the other students will be taking.

MS: Oh, I would never tell the others the questions in advance.

FP: (*Laughs*) I know you wouldn't. I always give different tests to students who have to take them at different times. I just want you to be aware that you will be taking an alternative test.

MS: Oh, of course! No problem. Thank you so much! I guess I'd better go and study for that final!

Narrator: Now get ready to answer the questions.

TRACK 3.31

Narrator: Listen to part of the lecture, and then answer the following question.

MS: Oh, I would never tell the others the questions in advance.

FP: (*Laughs*) I know you wouldn't.

Narrator: Why does the professor say this?

FP: (*Laughs*) I know you wouldn't.

TRACK 3.32

Narrator: Listen to part of a lecture in an archaeology class.

Male Professor (MP): So there have been many archaeological discoveries that have given us an idea of how people lived in the days before recorded history. One of the most significant of these discoveries is Chauvet Cave. The cave was discovered about 20 years ago, when three explorers moved the rock and debris that had been blocking the cave's entrance for about 25,000 years. So when they went into the cave, they stepped thousands of years into the past. The walls of the cave are covered in hundreds of well-preserved cave paintings, many of which are about 30,000 years old.

The paintings depict more than a dozen different animal species, and many of these are extinct today. One thing that really… (*To student*) Oh, you have a question?

Female Student (FS): Why did people make these drawings? Were they supposed to be practical, like a guide to hunting or something?

MP: Well, your question is one that researchers have been asking since the cave's discovery. Most researchers theorize that the drawings weren't meant to be hunting guides. Humans rarely hunted many of the animals depicted. In fact, one very unique feature of the art is that it shows a large number of predator species, including hyenas, bears, and lions. Much of the art discovered in other caves depicts mostly prey species, like mammoths and wild horses. So if the cave art at Chauvet is clearly different, it must have had a specific purpose. Let's go over some theories about why the artists created these paintings so many years ago….

Narrator: Now get ready to answer the questions.

CHAPTER 4

TRACK 4.01

Narrator: Listen to a lecture in a Greek mythology class.

Female Professor (FS): Ancient people used myths to explain the causes of natural phenomena such as rain, lightning, and even the movements of the sun and the stars. Today I'm going to talk about one of my favorite Greek myths: the kidnapping of Persephone. So I'll start by introducing the characters. Hades is the Greek god of the Underworld—in other words, he rules the kingdom that people go to after they die. And, because Hades' name is associated with death, he's not a well-liked god. Persephone is the daughter of Demeter, who is the goddess of earth, grain, and harvesting. Since the Greeks relied so heavily on farming, Demeter was an incredibly important and beloved goddess among the Greeks.

Now onto the story. One day, Hades left his kingdom in the Underworld to visit the surface world, where he saw the beautiful Persephone picking flowers in a field. Hades was struck by her beauty, so, instead of being polite and asking her out to dinner and a movie, he kidnapped Persephone and returned to the Underworld so they could be married.

After discovering that her beloved daughter had been kidnapped, Demeter demanded that Persephone be released, but Demeter's request was denied. In response, Demeter promised that she would not allow anything to grow on Earth until her daughter was returned. After much negotiation, Hades and Demeter came to an agreement: Persephone would live with Demeter for half the year and with Hades for the other half. When Persephone was with Hades for half the year, Demeter prevented anything from growing, which is how the Greeks explained the seasons of fall and winter. And when Persephone was with Demeter, she allowed crops to grow and flowers to bloom, explaining why plants grow so well in spring and summer.

Narrator: Now get ready to answer the questions

TRACK 4.02

Narrator: Listen to part of the lecture, and then answer the following question.
FP: Hades was struck by her beauty, so, instead of being polite and asking her out to dinner and a movie, he kidnapped Persephone and returned to the Underworld so they could be married.
Narrator: Why does the professor say this?
FP: Hades was struck by her beauty, so, instead of being polite and asking her out to dinner and a movie…

TRACK 4.03

Narrator: Listen to a lecture in an astronomy class.
Male Professor (MP): We've come to this location outside the city tonight to watch the motion of the stars in the sky. For thousands of years, people have noted that the stars appear to move across the night sky. But of course, stars don't really move around the Earth. The apparent movements of the stars are caused by the Earth's rotation around its own axis. And, just as a reminder, the Earth's axis is an imaginary line that the Earth spins around—the axis runs through the center of the Earth and emerges at the North and South Poles.

So now pretend that there are two points located very far away from Earth, but directly above the North and South Poles. These imaginary points are called the celestial poles, and the Earth's rotation makes it seem like all the stars in the night sky rotate around these poles. And this rotation causes stars to rise on the eastern horizon and descend below the western horizon, just like the Sun.

Now, because we are located in the Northern Hemisphere, finding the celestial pole is actually quite easy. All you have to do is look for Polaris, which is more commonly called the "North Star." This star is really close to the celestial north pole, so it doesn't appear to move like the other stars, and it's one of the brightest stars, making it pretty easy to find. In fact, before modern navigation equipment, sailors would use Polaris' fixed position for navigation, which is why some people call it the "Guiding Star."

Narrator: Now get ready to answer the questions.

TRACK 4.04

Narrator: Listen to a conversation between a student and an advisor.
Female Advisor (FA): Hi, Gordon. How'd you do on your GRE tests? Did you get a high enough score to enter the graduate program you want to apply for?
Male Student (MS): Well, I did pretty well on the general test. It's the third time I've taken it, you know.
FA: I know. You've been really committed to preparing for this test.
MS: But the English-literature subject test is a real pain. I've taken it twice and my score is still in the mid-level percentiles.
FA: I see. So, what type of score do you have to get on the subject test to enter your graduate program for English?
MS: Probably at least in the top ten percent.
FA: Wow, that will be difficult.

MS: Especially for English Literature. Do you realize that they can put any material from the whole history of English literature on the test?

FA: What will you do to prepare next time you take the test?

MS: Well, I've started reading anthologies that include the works of important English authors. Other than finishing those, I'm not sure what to do.

FA: Well, hang in there. Even if this one graduate program doesn't work out, there are always other grad programs you might like.

MS: You're probably right. In fact, I was just going over to the library to research other programs.

Narrator: Now get ready to answer the questions.

TRACK 4.05

Narrator: Listen to a lecture in an American history class.

Male Professor (MP): Today I'll be talking about the early history of the National Park System in the United States.

In the mid-1800s, hunters returned from the Yellowstone region, which is located in parts of Montana and Wyoming, with reports of strange natural wonders like massive hot springs, geysers, and even a mountain of black glass. So in 1870, a group of explorers undertook an expedition to visit the area and check the reports.

The expedition conducted a thorough investigation of the Yellowstone area by visiting geysers, observing wildlife, and climbing nearby mountains to get better views of the area. And after exploring the Yellowstone region, the expedition was able to confirm the reports: Yellowstone was, in fact, filled with all sorts of strange natural phenomena. Soon after the expedition, a man named Cornelius Hedges, who was a Montana lawyer and member of the Yellowstone expedition, said that the Yellowstone region should be preserved as a national park. Hedges promoted the national park idea by writing several articles for a Montana-based newspaper, giving lectures, and meeting with high government officials. Hedges' efforts succeeded in 1872, when President Ulysses Grant established Yellowstone National Park, the world's first national park. That's a pretty cool fact, huh: America is home to the oldest national park in the whole world. And then, during the 1890s, the National Parks System really picked up steam: four more national parks were established—Kings Canyon, Sequoia, and Yosemite in California, and Mount Rainier in Washington.

From these small beginnings came the hundreds of national parks we enjoy today.

Narrator: Now get ready to answer the questions.

TRACK 4.06

Narrator: What does the professor imply about Yellowstone when he says this?

MP: During the mid-1800s, hunters returned from the Yellowstone region with reports of strange natural wonders like massive hot springs, geysers, and a mountain of black glass.

TRACK 4.07

Narrator: Why does the professor say this?

MP: And then, during the 1890s, the National Parks System really picked up steam: four more national parks were established—Kings Canyon, Sequoia, and Yosemite in California, and Mount Rainier in Washington.

TRACK 4.08

Narrator: Listen to a conversation between a student and a professor.

Male Professor (MP): How can I help you, Kim?

Female Student (FS): I wanted to ask you about the "C" you gave me on my research paper. I was so bummed! I spent over a month on it.

MP: Well, I'm glad to hear you put a lot of effort into the paper. But that does not guarantee you a good grade.

FS: What do you mean?

MP: Let me look at your paper again. (*Reads paper*) First of all, you needed to include a bibliography. That was worth ten percent of your grade.

FS: But I put the names of the authors after each paragraph.

MP: Yes, but you need a bibliography at the end. We went over that in class.

FS: I remember now. But that still doesn't explain why I got a "C."

MP: Well, there's just not enough evidence to prove your thesis here.

FS: But my paper is ten pages long.

MP: Yes, but you repeat the same information over and over. See: on pages three, five, and seven you use nearly identical quotes.

FS: I see. I guess there's room for improvement.

MP: Always, Kim. Drop by my office before our next paper is due and I can give you some tips.

FS: Thanks, Professor Dawkins.

Narrator: Now get ready to answer the questions.

TRACK 4.09

Narrator: What can be inferred from this?

FS: I wanted to ask you about the "C" you gave me on my research paper. I was so bummed! I spent over a month on it.

TRACK 4.10

Narrator: Listen to a lecture in an American history class.

Female Professor (FP): Now let's move on to the structure of the American government. The U.S. government is divided into three major parts, which we call the three branches of government. And these three branches are the Executive Branch, the Legislative Branch, and the Judicial Branch.

The head of the Executive Branch is the President of the United States, and some of his duties include directing foreign affairs and approving of the decisions made by the Legislative Branch. The Legislative Branch consists of Congress, a group of politicians whose main job is to approve of or reject laws. And the Judicial Branch consists of the Supreme Court, which is a group of judges who review laws and make court decisions by interpreting the U.S. Constitution. (*To student*) Yes, what's your question?

Male Student (MS): But why are there three branches of government? Why not just combine all these branches into one group?

FP: Well, the U.S. was a group of British colonies before it became a country. But the colonists felt that the British king, who was basically in charge of the British government, was not giving them enough power or government representation. As a result, the colonists decided to break away from England and form their own nation, the United States. Naturally, the colonists in charge of structuring the U.S.

government wanted it to be different from the British monarchy, which was a government where the king had all the power. So the colonists carefully designed a government with three branches. That way, no one branch could control all the government's power: each branch exists to ensure that the other branches don't become too powerful. Basically, the three branches of U.S. government exist to make sure that the United States will never be ruled by a dictator, tyrant, or king.

Narrator: Now get ready to answer the questions.

TRACK 4.11

Narrator: What does the professor imply about the colonists that structured the U.S. government when she says this?

FP: Naturally, the colonists in charge of structuring the U.S. government wanted it to be different from the British monarchy, which was a government where the king had all the power. So the colonists carefully designed a government with three branches.

APPENDIX

Answer Key

CHAPTER 1

MAIN IDEA QUESTION - PRACTICE 1

Notes

stu. needs $ → wants on-campus job
advisor gives app. for dining hall job

1) C

When the advisor asks the student if he is looking for job openings, the student responds, "Yes, that's why I'm here." Thus, the conversation is about *on-campus job opportunities.*

MAIN IDEA QUESTION - PRACTICE 2

Notes

stu. asks prof. about harmonica hist.
prof. explains harmonica origins

2) D

The student and the professor are discussing the history of the harmonica, so the conversation is about *the origins of the harmonica.*

MAIN IDEA QUESTION - PRACTICE 3

Notes

stu. asks for prof. advice on taking a class
prof. tells her to take o-chem. first

3) A

The student wants to know if the professor thinks she is ready for a difficult, upper-division class. In other words, she asks him *if she should take a particular science class.*

MAIN IDEA QUESTION - PRACTICE 4

Notes

stu. wants to know how to become RA
UE says to fill out app. and wait for interview

4) A

The student wants to know how to become a resident assistant at the university, so the conversation is about *applying for a resident assistant position.*

DETAIL QUESTIONS - PRACTICE 1

Notes

stu. wants to know about a noise complaint he received in mailbox
→ noise complaints not serious
→ 3 noise complains = move out of dorms

1) C

The university employee tells the student that he must "leave the dorms" (*the student cannot live in the dorms*) if he receives three noise complaints.

2) D

The student states that he learned of the noise complain when he "received a letter in his campus mailbox."

DETAIL QUESTIONS - PRACTICE 2

Notes

stu. confused about lecture (Romantic lit.)
→ Romantic lit. = nature is vast, mystery
→ sci. rev. = nature can be understood

3) C

According to the student, the scientific revolution claimed that "everything about nature can be classified and understood." Thus, it emphasized *humanity's understanding of nature.*

4) A, D

The professor states, "Romantic literature really stresses the vastness (*immensity*) and mystery of nature."

DETAIL QUESTIONS - PRACTICE 3

Notes

stu. wants to learn about loans, grants, scholarships
→ loan = gov. $ that must be paid back
→ grant = gov. $ for poor
→ scholarship = $ for acad. achievement

5) B

The advisor states that grants "go to U.S. citizens who need financial aid to attend college," *so students who need financial assistance.*

6) D

The advisor states that a loan is government money that must be paid back, while a grant is government money that students do not need to pay back.

DETAIL QUESTIONS - PRACTICE 4

Notes

stu. wants to know about downsides of transferring unis.
→ *wants to transfer to Upstate Uni. for robotics, would have to retake GEs*
→ *current major = electrical engineer*

7) A

Although she mentions looking at coast University and United University, the student claims, "I want to transfer to Upstate University…"

8) C

When asked what her current major is, the student states, "It's electrical engineering."

PURPOSE QUESTIONS - PRACTICE 1

Notes

stu. needs to find engineering books
→ *lib. tells stu. he's in wrong library; tells stu. to walk to diff. library*

1) C

Based on the conversation, the student approaches the librarian in order to ask "where the books on engineering are."

2) A

The student mentions that it is her first time in the library to explain why she cannot find the engineering books, so she is explaining why *she needs* the librarian's *help*.

PURPOSE QUESTIONS - PRACTICE 2

Notes

stu. wants prof. to recommend anthro./myth books
→ *Prof. mentions Golden Bough (Frazer), says it's dated but interesting*

3) B

In the conversation, the student immediately asks the professor for "any book recommendations."

4) D

An anthropology book "that covers pretty basic concepts" is one that does not go into detail, making it suitable for someone who is unfamiliar with the subject. Thus, we can conclude that the student *does not know a lot about anthropology.*

PURPOSE QUESTIONS - PRACTICE 3

Notes

stu. wants to return lib. books
→ *lib. tells him they're overdue*
→ *stu. misunderstands library policy, can only keep books for 2 weeks*

5) D

The student gives his purpose for talking to the librarian when he says, "I'd like to return these library books…"

6) A

Here, the student is explaining why he kept the books for weeks after their due dates, so he is explaining *why he turned the books in late.*

PURPOSE QUESTIONS - PRACTICE 4

Notes

stu. wants to know about dog intelligence
→ *introduces question by mentioning her exp. w/ collies & poodles*
prof. recommends book

7) B

The student asks the professor about "the intelligence of different types of dogs," so her purpose for visiting the professor is *to ask about studies on dog intelligence.*

8) C

The student starts the conversation by talking about her personal experience with certain types of dogs. Afterward, she asks a question that relates to her personal experience.

INFERENCE QUESTIONS - PRACTICE 1

Notes

stu. asks prof. about history of singing in the bathroom, stu. enjoys singing
→ *prof. says that musicians noticed same (ex. Simon and Garfunkel)*

1) A

The student says, "I often find myself singing in the shower," so we can infer that *he enjoys singing in his free time* because he does so often.

2) B

The professor gives the student background information about the practice of singing in the shower. Thus, she is being *informative* throughout the conversation.

INFERENCE QUESTIONS - PRACTICE 2

Notes

stu. wants to know about structure of final exam
→ prof. doesn't know details yet
→ will include translation portion

3) C

We can infer that the student is relieved because she says that the test sounds easier than she thought it would be.

4) A

Had the professor already created the final exam, he would know exactly what he included on the test. Since he says that he is "not exactly sure what will be on the exam," we can infer that *he has not created* it yet.

INFERENCE QUESTIONS - PRACTICE 3

Notes

stu. talks to prof. about project
→ stu. having trouble with conclusion (unhappy)
→ prof. gives advice, stu. satisfied

5) B

Because the student does not know how to complete a major part of his project, we can infer that he is *frustrated*.

6) D

After the professor gives the student advice, the student says, "I think you just saved my project!" Thus, the student will probably complete his project by *following the professor's suggestions*.

INFERENCE QUESTIONS - PRACTICE 4

Notes

stu. wants to switch majors (sociology to bio.)
→ advisor gives stu. form; head of bio. dpt. must sign
→ stu. to return to advisor w/ signed form

7) A

The advisor demonstrates a *supportive* attitude throughout the conversation, such as when he assures the student that "switching majors is a pretty easy process."

8) C

After handing the student a form, the advisor tells her to first "have the head of the biology department" sign it. Thus, we can infer that she will *visit the head of the biology department* after the conversation.

Exercise 1

Notes

stu. looking for book of sheet music for class
→ bookstore sold out of book
emp. recommends 2 solutions:
   1) wait for new shipment of books
   2) get book at nearby store
stu. will try to find book at nearby store

Multiple-Choice Answers

1) D

Inference Question

Because the employee mentions that he works in "the textbook section of the store," and because the main topic of the conversation is a specific book, we can infer that the conversation takes place in *a bookstore*.

2) C

Detail Question

The student states that she cannot find *a book of sheet music* that she needs for one of her classes.

3) B

Detail Question

The employee says that he has seen the book that the student is looking for "at the record store down the street." So he is recommending that the student *go to the record store* to find the book.

4) C

Inference Question

The employee claims that he is "a classical music buff," so we can infer that he *is knowledgeable about classical music*.

5) A

Inference Question

We can infer that the student was *grateful* for the employees help because she thanks him at the end of the conversation.

Exercise 2

Notes

man wants to apply to the uni., in wrong office
advisor gives man directions to Registrar's
→ man in Financial Aid Office
man given financial aid packet

Multiple-Choice Answers

1) B

   Main Idea Question

   The main reason that the man talks to the advisor is that he wants to learn how to *apply to the university*.

2) A

   Detail Question

   After the man says that he wants to apply to the university, the advisor tells him, "…this is the Financial Aid Office."

3) B

   Detail Question

   When the advisor is giving the man directions, she says, "I'll circle the Registrar's on the map for you."

4) D

   Inference Question

   With his comment, the man is implying that he will probably need financial assistance to pay the university's tuition. Thus, we can infer that tuition at the university is *expensive*.

5) C

   Inference Question

   After the conversation, the man will probably go to the Registrar's Office, which is next to the library. Since the library "is about one-hundred yards north" of the man's current location, we can infer that he will *walk north*.

Exercise 3

Notes

stu. lost ID, needs replacement
→ required: pic. ID, $15
stu. thinks replacement too much $
→ ↑ price to prevent stu. from losing ID
stu. going to dorm for ID, $

Multiple-Choice Answers

1) C

   Main Idea Question

   The first statement the student makes—that *he lost his student ID and needs a new one*—reveals the main purpose of the conversation.

2) D

   Inference Question

   Because he refers to the student ID as "a little piece of plastic," we can infer that he believes the IDs are not worth 15 dollars, meaning that the new ID is *too expensive*.

3) A, C

   Detail Question

   The employee tells the student that she needs "to see some other form of picture ID," and that "it costs 15 dollars to print a new student ID."

4) B

   Detail Question

   The advisor tells the student that the university charges 15 dollars to replace a student ID "to discourage students from losing their IDs…"

5) D

   Inference Question

   At the end of the conversation, the student says, "I'll be back with my license and 15 dollars in a few minutes," so we can infer that he will get *his driver's license and money from his room* after the conversation.

Exercise 4

Notes

stu. wants internship; needs letter of rec.
→ internship competitive
prof. agrees to write letter
internship on spectro., prof. says its interesting
→ letter of rec. ready by Mon.

Multiple-Choice Answers

1) B

   Main Idea Question

   The student mentions that she wants the professor to write her a letter of recommendation so she can apply to a competitive internship.

2) D

   Detail Question

   At the beginning of the conversation, the professor says, "summer internships can be really helpful for gaining practical lab experience." Thus, he believes that *they are often very helpful*.

3) A

Detail Question

Toward the end of the conversation, the professor says, "...I'll have the letter of recommendation ready by Monday."

4) B

Inference Question

The professor says to the student, "You've always turned in excellent work," and we can infer that the student's quality work is a result of her *working hard in her classes*.

5) A

Inference Question

After the student describes the summer internship, the professor says, "That should be interesting." Thus, the professor believes that the internship *will probably be interesting*.

Exercise 5

Notes

no Internet in dorm
→ *stu. asked others, restart comp.*
→ *advisor sending repair person to check*
advisor tells student to work in lib., Internet OK there
advisor will email when Internet OK in dorm

Multiple-Choice Answers

1) C

Main Idea Question

The reason that the student visits the employee is to state that he "can't seem to get on the Internet" (*he cannot access the Internet*) in his dorm.

2) B, D

Detail Question

The student tells the employee that he has "asked others" in his building if they have Internet access, and he says that he has "tried restarting" his computer.

3) A

Purpose Question

Because the student mentions his report only after asking if the Internet will be operational soon, we can infer that he mentions the report *to explain his sense of urgency*.

4) C

Detail Question

The employee tells the student, "I'll have to send one of our repair people to check on the school's wireless Internet system." Thus, she helps the student by *promising to contact a repair person*.

5) B

Inference Question

The employee says that the library is "quiet" and that "the Internet is working fine there." With these comments, the employee is implying that the library *is a convenient place to write reports*.

CHAPTER 2

MAIN IDEA QUESTION - PRACTICE 1

Notes

depression affects 7-10% of U.S.
→ *different from sadness, affects all parts of life*
→ *no simple treatment, many risk factors*

1) B

After introducing the topic of depression, the professor spends most of the lecture differentiating temporary sadness and depression.

MAIN IDEA QUESTION - PRACTICE 2

Notes

topic = origins of flag
→ *Roman flag = vexillum, for military*
→ *later Euro. flags based on vexillum*

2) A

The professor introduces the lecture by saying, "I'd like to get into the origins of the flag," and he focuses on the history of the flag as it was developed *in Europe*.

MAIN IDEA QUESTION - PRACTICE 3

Notes

topic = ancient use of salt
→ *salt once very valuable, used as preservative*
→ *word "salary" refers to salt payment*

3) C

The professor presents the main idea of the lecture when she says, "salt was once much more valuable than it is today." Thus, the lecture is mainly about *the importance of salt in ancient times*.

MAIN IDEA QUESTION - PRACTICE 4

Notes

diesel engines very efficient
→ *air is compressed, then fuel added; combustion creates energy*

4) D

Throughout the lecture, the professor explains why "the diesel engine is the most efficient" type of engine.

DETAIL QUESTIONS - PRACTICE 1

Notes

Georgia = impt. U.S. state
→ *Atlanta = capital, largest city in state; lots of commerce & financial*

1) D

The professor mentions that Georgia "plays a big role in the economy," meaning it is an important business center, and she says that Georgia has "urban manufacturing centers," so it is an *important area for manufacturing*.

2) A, B

The professor says that Atlanta "is Georgia's capital and the state's largest city."

DETAIL QUESTIONS - PRACTICE 2

Notes

banjo = American folk instrument
→ *played like guitar, from Africa*
→ *many names, T. Jefferson commented on skill of South. black players*

3) B

At the beginning of the lecture, the professor describes the banjo as "an instrument that is very much a part of American folk music."

4) D

At the end of the lecture, the professor says that Thomas Jefferson "remarked on the impressive skills of black banjo players," so *he commented on the talent of black banjo players*.

DETAIL QUESTIONS - PRACTICE 3

Notes

most people think wasps = aggressive, painful stings
but really, wasps = eat insects that eat crops, pollinate flowers/crops, only sting when angered

5) A

The professor claims that most people think a wasp is "an aggressive" insect (*easily* angered) with "a sharp, painful sting" (*deliver painful stings*).

6) C, D

When listing the helpful qualities of wasps, the professor says that wasps "prey on insects that are harmful to crops," and they "feed on nectar, which helps with pollination…" (*pollinate flowers*).

DETAIL QUESTIONS - PRACTICE 4

Notes

public housing = for poor
  1) gov. manages apt. buildings, charges ↓ rent, many built in 1950s & 1960s, too much crime here
  2) gov. gives "vouchers" for private apts., more job opportunities

7) B, C

According to the passage, the government houses the poor (1) by managing "public apartment buildings" (*building public housing*), and (2) by providing "'vouchers' to help pay rent for private apartments" (*providing rent vouchers*).

8) D

At the end of the lecture, the professor says that living in private apartments "may help people move to neighborhoods where there are more opportunities, especially for jobs."

PURPOSE QUESTIONS - PRACTICE 1

Notes

coffee has caffeine
caffeine boosts nervous system, ↑ energy, ↑ motor skills
some can't sleep after coffee, some can

1) D

Shortly after mentioning coffee, the professor discusses the effects of a chemical in coffee called "caffeine." Thus, we can infer that she mentions coffee *to discuss the chemical effects* that it has on people.

2) A

Throughout the lecture, the professor discuses the effects of coffee on the body, so we can conclude that the statement, "coffee causes sleeplessness" describes another *potential side effect of coffee drinking*.

PURPOSE QUESTIONS - PRACTICE 2

Notes

differences bet. African & Asian elephants
→ *African = 4 toenails, bigger ears, tusks*
→ *Asian = 5 toenails, most no tusks*
cannot interbreed (only crossbreed died)

3) B

The professor says, "African elephants have much larger ears than Asian elephants," so he mentions ears *to describe a difference between* the two types of elephant.

4) A

The professor explains that the attempt to crossbreed an Asian and African elephant failed because "they are too genetically different." Thus, the crossbred elephant is mentioned *to emphasize the genetic differences between* the two types of elephant.

PURPOSE QUESTIONS - PRACTICE 3

Notes

history of daylight savings
→ *first suggested by B. Franklin*
→ *used in all U.S. b/c of Uniform Time Act (1966)*

5) B

The professor says that daylight savings "was first suggested by... Benjamin Franklin," so the professor is connecting Franklin to *the origins of daylight savings*.

6) A

After mentioning the Uniform Time Act, the professor says, "And I can tell you from first-hand experience..." so we can conclude that he is *sharing a personal experience*.

PURPOSE QUESTIONS - PRACTICE 4

Notes

layout of Greek theaters
→ *open, seat up to 20,000, acting space = orchestra*
→ *very good acoustics to carry actors voices*

7) D

The professor discusses "the architecture of ancient Greek theaters," which includes descriptions of many *unique features* of these structures.

8) C

The professor's example of dropping a pin demonstrates that a small sound can be heard through the entire theater, so the example shows *how clear the acoustics in a Greek theater are*.

INFERENCE QUESTIONS - PRACTICE 1

Notes

myths = kind of like history
→ *M. Eliade = myth are altered reality*
  (prof. agrees w/ this claim)

1) D

The professor starts the lecture by stating that most people equate myths with fiction. He then claims that myths are "altered accounts of real events," so *they contain more truth than most people realize*.

2) A

The phrase "...I am fully with her..." implies that the professor supports or *agrees with Mircea Eliade's view*.

INFERENCE QUESTIONS - PRACTICE 2

Notes

American lit. from 1600s from North, religious, from cities most Southerners farmers, isolated, ↓ lit.
→ *in 1800s, South produced much lit ("fruit" = lit.)*

3) A, D

The professor says that, during the 17th and 18th centuries, "most American literature came from the Northern colonies," and that this literature was "religious in nature."

4) D

Here, the professor is comparing literary production to agriculture. Thus, the "drought" is the lack of Southern literature, and the "fruit" are works of literature. The professor is implying that, starting in the 19th century, the South *produced many great writers*.

INFERENCE QUESTIONS - PRACTICE 3

Notes

can dinosaurs see color?
→ birds = dino. relatives; birds see color
  (evolved under diff. conditions)
→ dinos. have big eyes & optic lobes, vision impt. to them
still debate about topic

5) B

The professor starts the lecture by mentioning "one of the many questions that paleontologists wonder…" and then he presents theories *that attempt to explain* the question.

6) D

A "heated debate" implies that people still disagree about dinosaur vision, so the professor is saying that people *are uncertain whether or not dinosaurs saw color*.

INFERENCE QUESTIONS - PRACTICE 4

Notes

plastic: over 50 types (more being developed), versatile material
→ often strong, light, sturdy, cheap

7) D

Because the professor says, "most of us come into contact with [plastic] every day of our lives," we can infer that plastic *is necessary for everyday life*.

8) C

Because plastic is a "versatile material," we can infer that it is *used in many products for different industries*.

Exercise 1

Notes

vitamins = compounds not produced by body, need to be eaten
→ necessary vitamins differ from organism to organism
Vitamin C: most produce, primates (humans) need to eat.
next: what vitamins do

Multiple-Choice Answers

1) A

Main Idea Question

At the beginning of the lecture, the professor says, "I want to begin talking about vitamins. He then spends the lecture describing some important *qualities of vitamins*.

2) D

Purpose Question

The professor is saying that the student's answer was "more or less" correct, which means that *the student's response was mostly correct*.

3) C

Detail Question

The professor describes a vitamin as "a substance that an organism doesn't produce naturally, so it needs to get that compound from its environment," so a vitamin is *a compound not produced in the body*.

4) A

Detail Question

According to the professor, "most animals and pretty much all plants produce Vitamin C naturally…"

5) B

Detail Question

Toward the end of the lecture, the professor says that "primates, including humans, must eat food with Vitamin C in it to survive."

6) D

Inference Question

At the end of the lecture, the professor says that the class will discuss "the role of Vitamin C in the human body." Thus, the class will talk about *the functions of vitamins in the body*.

Exercise 2

Notes

Adam Smith (econ. father); 1776 → Wealth of Nations
everyone must pursue own success
→ ex. shoemaker sells @ highest $, buys food @ lowest $
→ bargaining = cooperation, everyone gets what they need
→ "invisible hand"
bad = people conspire to raise prices
→ disrupt balance, gov. has to regulate

Multiple-Choice Answers

1) D

Main Idea Question
The professor introduces Adam Smith, in the first sentence of the lecture, and she spends the rest of the lecture describing *Adam Smith's theories*.

2) A

Inference Question
According to the lecture, Smith thought that "bargaining is a form of cooperation among people," so we can infer that *he encouraged it*.

3) B

Purpose Question
The professor describes the part of the lecture about the shoemaker as a "simple example," so the shoemaker's bargaining is *an example of something supported by Smith*.

4) C

Purpose Question
According to the professor, "people are 'led by an invisible hand'" in "free and fair markets."

5) C

Purpose Question
Because the professor refutes what "some people" believe about Smith, we can infer that the professor is *correcting a common misconception*.

6) A

Detail Question
At the end of the lecture, the professor says, "the government must watch the marketplaces carefully." In other words, Smith believed that the government *should oversee markets*.

Exercise 3

Notes

differences bet. mass & weight
→ *mass = amount of matter in something; if touchable, then mass*
→ *weight = gravity's pull on something*
ex: prof. in spaceship: farther from Earth → less gravity
→ *less weight*

Multiple-Choice Answers

1) D

Main Idea Question
Throughout the lecture, the professor discusses the "completely different meanings" of the terms "mass" and "weight."

2) B

Detail Question
According to the professor, "people often use the terms 'mass' and 'weight' as if they have the same meaning," so the terms *are often used interchangeably*.

3) C

Purpose Question
Here, the professor is describing the relationship between "anything you can touch" and "mass." Thus, the phrase "anything you can touch" *describes a general characteristic of* mass.

4) A

Inference Question
Immediately after defining "weight," he *gives an example about traveling in a spaceship* that illustrates differences between weight and mass.

5) A

Detail Question
The professor claims that, as he flew away from "Earth's gravitational pull" in a spaceship, he would come to "weigh as little as the surrounding air."

6) D

Inference Question
Because weight is affected by gravitational pull, but mass is not, we can infer that *an object's mass does not change based on location* but its weight does.

Exercise 4

Notes

phantom limb syndrome = feels like missing limb attached
→ *occurs among 80% of amputee patients*
→ *some ideas, but cause unknown*
prof. asks for class' opinions on cause
→ *maybe in brain*

Multiple-Choice Answers

1) D

Main Idea Question
The main topic of the lecture is phantom limb syndrome, and the professor says that the causes of the syndrome "remain a mystery." Thus, the professor

is talking about *an unexplained physical sensation.*

2) C

Purpose Question

Here, the professor defines the term "phantom," and then she clarifies that she is *using the term "phantom" differently than students might expect.*

3) D

Detail Question

About midway through the lecture, the professor reveals that "up to 80 percent of amputee patients report having phantom limb sensations."

4) A

Detail Question

According to the lecture, phantom limb syndrome "becomes a real medical concern when people report feeling pain" in a missing limb (*phantom limb pain*).

5) A

Inference Question

The professor begins the lecture by *describing phantom limb syndrome*, and then she notes that some people with this syndrome experience a sensation called *phantom limb pain.*

6) B

Inference Question

We can infer that the professor associates phantom limb syndrome with *the brain* because she asks, "…which areas of the brain might possibly be responsible for this [phantom limb] sensation?"

Exercise 5

Notes

Alaska Purchase (1867) bet. U.S. & Russia
→ *made by Sec. of State Seward; bought for $7.2 mil, some thought waste of $*
→ *good purchase, Alaska has oil, gold*
Russia sold to U.S. as a buffer from British Canada

Multiple-Choice Answers

1) B

Main Idea Question

Throughout the lecture, the professor discusses the Alaska Purchase by explaining *how and why Alaska became a part of the U.S.*

2) C

Detail Question

The professor says that some Americans opposed the Alaska Purchase because they thought that "the U.S. government needed to spend its money on rebuilding its war-torn communities" after the Civil War.

3) A

Inference Question

The professor says that those who opposed the Alaska Purchase "silenced themselves" when Alaska proved profitable. Thus, we can conclude that those who opposed the purchase *changed their minds.*

4) D

Purpose Question

The professor reveals that Russia sold Alaska because "Russian rulers worried that they would not be able to defend the territory" from neighboring British Canada. Thus, clarifying that Canada belonged to Britain *explain why Russia decided to sell Alaska.*

5) B

Detail Question

The professor reveals that Russia sold Alaska because "Russian rulers worried that they would not be able to defend the territory" from British Canada (Alaska *would be difficult to protect*).

6) C

Inference Question

Because Russia's main motivation for selling Alaska to the U.S. was to "help control British power," we can infer that both Russia and the U.S. hoped to *stop British expansion.*

CHAPTER 3

ACTUAL PRACTICE 1 - PRACTICE SET 1

Notes

modernist designs (simple design, mass-produce); affordable, useful
Germany = Bauhaus (early 1900s)
  1) *wallpaper = prime. colors, geo. shapes, cheap wall decoration*
  2) *M. Breuer = bike armchair (steel tubing); cheap, practical*
next: art inspired by Bauhaus

Multiple Choice Answers

1) D

Main Idea Question

The professor begins the lecture by introducing modernist designs, but he spends the majority of the lecture discussing *one highly influential school for modernist designs* called "Bauhaus."

2) B

Detail Question

According to the professor, Bauhaus "was a special trade school in Germany."

3) A

Inference Question

According to the professor, "modernist design aimed for very simple forms that could be mass-produced in factories." Thus, we can infer that modernist designers valued factories, so they probably believed that industrialization could lead to a better society.

4) D

Inference Question

Bicycles are very common objects, and a Bauhaus designer was inspired to design a chair using bicycle parts. Thus, we can infer that Bauhaus *art was sometimes inspired by everyday objects*.

5) C

Inference Question

Because the professor emphasizes the practicality and affordability of Bauhaus designs, we can infer that he is *respectful* when discussing the Bauhaus school's designs.

6) B

Inference Question

At the end of the lecture, the professor says, "let's talk about some other modernist design schools whose designs were influenced by the Bauhaus," so the class will discuss *design school that drew inspiration from the Bauhaus school*.

ACTUAL PRACTICE 1 - PRACTICE SET 2

Notes

student wants to become newspaper intern
→ internship → uni. credit, no $
student = Eng. major, writes for school paper; wants work exp. as journalist
→ student must talk to Dr. Henry, complete application, be interviewed, bring writing samples

Multiple-Choice Answers

1) C

Detail Question

The employee introduces herself by saying, "this is the *Daily Tribune Newspaper*'s publishing office," so she must work at *a newspaper publisher*.

2) A

Purpose Question

The student says that he wants to intern at the newspaper publisher because he's "hoping to become a journalist after" graduating college (*to explore a future career*).

3) B

Detail Question

When the employee asks the student if he is "majoring in journalism at the moment," the student responds by says, "No, in English." Thus, the student is studying *English*.

4) A

Detail Question

Shortly after mentioning Dr. Henry, the employee tells the student to "fill out an application form with him."

5) C

Detail Question

After scheduling an interview with the student, the employee tells him to "bring a couple samples of your writing."

ACTUAL PRACTICE 1 - PRACTICE SET 3

Notes

history of the button
→ prehistoric times: made of bone, shell, wood; only decoration
→ 13th c. Europe: buttons fasten, tighter fashion, pushed through loops
→ 1800s: buttons manufactured, more can afford

Multiple-Choice Answers

1) A

Main Idea Question

Since the lecture begins by discussing the use of buttons in prehistoric times, and concludes by discussing the manufacture of modern buttons, we can conclude that the subject of the lecture is *how buttons have affected fashion throughout history*.

2) B

Detail Question

The professor states, "Even in prehistoric times, people made buttons out of bones, shells, or wood."

3) C

Purpose Question

According to the professor, buttons allowed people to "wear fashions that were pulled tightly from shoulder to hip," so buttons *fastened clothing more effectively.*

4) D

Inference Question

The professor says that the factory-produced "metal buttons with four holes in the center" are still being used today, so we can infer that this button design *was so popular that it remains the standard flat shape.*

5)

1)	C
2)	B
3)	D
4)	A

Inference Question

During "prehistoric times, people made buttons out of bones, shells, or wood." Then, during the 13th century, use of buttons allowed people "to wear fashions that were pulled tightly from shoulder to hip." By the 1800s, "factories began producing flat metal buttons." The low cost of producing these buttons "allowed more men and women to wear… tight-fitting fasions…."

ACTUAL PRACTICE 2 - PRACTICE SET 1

Notes

topic = *fugue structure*
→ *fugue = (1) subject, (2) answer, (3) repeat*
→ *melody, key changes as its repeated*
→ *exposition = 1st part of fugue*
→ *develop. epi. = 2nd part of fugue*

Multiple Choice Answers

1) D

Main Idea Question

The main topic of the lecture is the structure of a fugue, which "is a type of [musical] composition."

2) C

Detail Question

After the professor asks, "…which instrument played the subject melody?" a student correctly answers that "it was a violin."

3) A

Detail Question

The professor remarks that the answer melody played by the flute was "repeated in a different musical key" than the subject melody.

4) D

Inference Question

The male student remarks, "there is something different about the melody the flute played," and the professor confirms that the answer melody is in a different key than the subject melody. Thus, we can infer that a fugue's melody *changes as different instruments play it.*

5) B

Inference Question

All of the professor's questions test the students' knowledge regarding the structure of a fugue. From this, we can conclude that the professor wants to ensure that *her students understand the lecture information.*

6) B

Inference Question

Immediately after mentioning "developmental episodes," the professor says, "We'll talk about that in just a little while," so the class will discuss *developmental episodes* next.

ACTUAL PRACTICE 2 - PRACTICE SET 2

Notes

man received an "F" in chem. class
man got "A"s on all assignments; "F" = mistake
→ *prof. in Germany now; solution: get profs. phone #*
→ *students going to chem. dept.*
man tone = upset
woman tone = concerned

Multiple-Choice Answers

1) B

Inference Question

At the beginning of the conversation, the woman says to the man, "You look like you're about to cry." Thus, we can infer that he is *upset* during the conversation.

2) B

Detail Question

The woman states that she got "straight 'Bs'" on her report card. Thus, we can conclude that she got a "*B*" in her chemistry class.

3) D

Inference Question

The woman says that the man "got 'As' on every test and project" in his chemistry class, and she claims that she "probably would have gotten an 'F'" in the class without his help. Thus, we can infer that *he knows a lot about chemistry*.

4) A

Detail Question

The woman advises the man to "call and explain the [grade] situation to" his professor in Germany (*Contact Professor Keller*).

5) B

Inference Question

When the woman recommends that the man go to the chemistry department to ask for his professor's phone number, he says, "I guess you're right. Will you walk over there with me?" Thus, we can infer that, after the conversation, the speakers will *go to the chemistry department*.

ACTUAL PRACTICE 2 - PRACTICE SET 3

Notes

classical conditioning (ex. banana cream pie)
→ *Pavlov dog: bell + food = mouth water → bell = mouth water (ex. of conditioning)*
→ *Watson: Albert + rat = happy → Albert + rat + loud noise = scared → Albert + rat = scared*
→ *past experiences condition future responses*

Multiple-Choice Answers

1) D

Main Idea Question

The professor reveals the main topic of the lecture immediately by saying, "Today's topic is classical conditioning."

2) A

Purpose Question

After discussing people's possible reactions to banana cream pie, he states, "past experiences *condition* our responses." Thus, the example involving pie serves *to introduce the topic of conditioning*.

3) B

Detail Question

According to the professor, "the dogs' mouths would water when they heard the signal…"

4) C

Detail Question

The professor explains that, ultimately, Watson's experiment caused Albert to be "*conditioned* to fear rats," so Watson *conditioned a child to fear an animal*.

5) D

Detail Question

According to the professor, little Albert "associated the rat with the frightening noise."

6) A

Inference Question

Because the professor says that Watson's experiment is "unethical because of how poor little Albert was treated," we can infer that the professor *believes the experiment was harmful to little Albert*.

ACTUAL PRACTICE 3 - PRACTICE SET 1

Notes

Hieronymus Bosch paintings
Bosch = 15th c. Netherlands
→ *inspired by proverbs, Bible, astro., named after city*
triptych = three connected paintings
Tempt. of St. Anthony = about saint resisting temptation.
next will talk about sig. of chars. in painting

Multiple-Choice Answers

1) B

Main Idea Question

The professor mainly talks about Hieronymus Bosch (*a famous painter*), who was active during the Renaissance period.

2) A

Detail Question

According to the professor, "Bosch was influenced by a variety of sources, including Dutch proverbs, Biblical stories, and astrology."

3) C

Purpose Question

Here, the professor is describing some features (*identifying characteristics*) present in much of Bosch's art.

4) A

Inference Question

Because Bosch waned to emphasize "Anthony's ability to...reject all this corruption and greed," we can infer that Bosch is *depicting Saint Anthony as a good, virtuous man* who can resist temptation.

5) 's-Hertogenbosch — A

Triptych — C

The Temptation of Saint Anthony — B

Inference Question

According to the professor, *'s-Hertogenbosch* is "the name of the town in the Netherlands where Bosch was born." A *triptych* is "three related paintings that are mounted on wood panels...." And *The Temptation of Saint Anthony* is a painting about a man who "rejects...[the] corruption and greed that surrounds him."

ACTUAL PRACTICE 3 - PRACTICE SET 2

Notes

Woman worried abt. failing calc.

man recommends tutoring center

→ woman worries tutors not helpful

→ man received good tutor help for writing

man will walk w/ woman to tutoring center

Multiple-Choice Answers

1) B

Detail Question

At the beginning of the lecture, the woman says, "these calculus problems just don't make any sense to me," so we can conclude that she is studying *calculus*.

2) A

Inference Question

At the beginning of the conversation, the woman is having trouble with her calculus assignment, and she claims, "I just don't know what to do." From this information, we can infer that she is *frustrated*.

3) D

Detail Question

After the woman expresses her frustration, the man tells her, "Maybe you should try the university tutoring center."

4) D

Inference Question

After the man mentions his poor writing skills during his freshman year, the woman says to the man, "You thought you might have to drop out of the university because of your grades." Thus, we can infer that the man *had difficulty with his classes as a freshman*.

5) B

Inference Question

At the end of the conversation, the man suggests that he walk with the woman to the tutoring center. Because the woman says, "sounds like a good idea," we can infer that the woman will *go to the tutoring center*.

ACTUAL PRACTICE 3 - PRACTICE SET 3

Notes

Realist literature

→ *Realism = 1800s, portray real life; revolt against Classic./Romantic.*

→ *Realists try to leave their opinions out, but always some*

→ *themes = upbringing, minorities, values*

lecture organization = define → origins → examples

Multiple-Choice Answers

1) A

Main Idea Question

The professor describes the main topic, Realism, as being "so widespread in today's fiction and drama that it is no longer recognized as a distinct artistic movement." Thus, we can conclude that Realism is *influential* and an *artistic and literary movement*.

2) B

Detail Question

According to the professor, Realism is "widespread in today's fiction and drama," so *it is still popular in drama and fiction*.

3) C

Detail Question

The professor states, "A Realist author's main goal is to describe, as accurately as possible, what is perceived through the senses."

4) B

Purpose Question

Because the professor states that "Realism started out as a revolt..." against other artistic movements, we can infer that the excerpt *explains why Realism developed*.

5) C

Detail Question

The professor says, "Common Realist themes today include the importance of upbringing…"

6) A

Inference Question

Toward the end of the lecture, the professor describes several themes in Realist literature, then she says, "You'll see all of these [themes] illustrated… in *The Jungle*." Thus, we can infer that *The Jungle is a Realist work of literature* because it contains many Realist themes.

ACTUAL PRACTICE 4 - PRACTICE SET 1

Notes

contagious yawning (in apes, wolves, dogs)
main question: "Why do we yawn?"
→ links to empathy (brain scans)
→ soc. mammals have to understand e/o
understand yawning → understand empathy

Multiple-Choice Answers

1) C

Main Idea Question

Shortly after asking the lecture's "focus question," the professor reveals the main topic of the lecture: the idea that "researchers think that 'contagious yawning' has something to do with empathy."

2) A

Inference Question

After the professor states that "talking about yawning… can make us [other people] want to yawn as well," she notices that some students are "affected" by what she says. Thus, we can infer that her *talking about yawning has made some students yawn.*

3) C, D

Detail Question

The professor says, "contagious yawning ahs been observed among… some apes, wolves, and dogs."

4) D

Purpose Question

According to the professor, brain scans show "that yawning activates the same area of the brain as empathy and social knowledge," so brain scans are mentioned to *introduce evidence that yawning and empathy are linked.*

5) B

Detail Question

The professor claims that social species must communicate and cooperate in order "to find food and defend territory."

6) C

Inference Question

The professor begins the lecture by discussing the significance of yawning (*a phenomenon*), and then she connects it to the *larger research topic* of the connection between empathy and yawning.

ACTUAL PRACTICE 4 - PRACTICE SET 2

Notes

woman trying to arrange transport for museum trip
→ visiting Museum of Contemp. Art
→ woman asks man if he needs ride
→ man accepts ride
man will ask Alicia if she needs ride
→ will ask her in upcoming class

Multiple-Choice Answers

1) C

Main Idea Question

The woman offers the man a ride for a class trip. Because this remains the main topic throughout the conversation, we can conclude that the conversation is about *organizing transportation for a class trip.*

2) B

Detail Question

At the beginning of the conversation, the woman asks that man if he is "going to the Museum of Contemporary Art for Dr. Tatum's class…."

3) D

Detail Question

After the man says that his friend, Alicia, might need a ride to the museum, he says, "I don't have her phone number."

4) A

Inference Question

Since both speakers want to go to the museum for Dr. Tatum's class, we can infer that they are in that class together. Thus, they probably *know each other from Dr. Tatum's class.*

5) C

Inference Question

At the end of the conversation, the man says, "I've got to go to class."

ACTUAL PRACTICE 4 - PRACTICE SET 3

Notes
some bacteria harmful
bacteria outnumber human cells in body (10:1)
→ bacteria all over us
→ very small, get into us in food & drink
→ some help digestion, some help fight bad bacteria

Multiple-Choice Answers

1) C

   Main Idea Question

   After introducing the subject of bacteria, the professor introduces the main topic—the idea that, in the human body, "bacteria outnumber human cells at a ratio that could be as high as 10 to 1."

2) B

   Purpose Question

   The professor begins the lecture by mentioning the harmful bacteria that most people are familiar with, but he does so *to contrast them with harmless and beneficial bacteria*, which he spends most of the lecture discussing.

3) A

   Inference Question

   We can assume that most people believe that, in the human body, human cells outnumber bacteria. Thus, it may surprise people to learn that bacteria actually outnumber human cells, so *human bodies contain more bacteria than many people realize*.

4) D

   Detail Question

   The professor says that, because of bacteria's small size, they "don't take up too much space in our bodies."

5) A

   Inference Question

   The professor says that bacteria are transferred to our bodies "during breastfeeding... [and] from the food you eat and the water you drink." Because these are all common human actions, we can infer that the professor believes that acquiring bacteria is *natural and ordinary*.

6) A, C

   Detail Question

   According to the professor, bacteria "help us get more energy from our food," and they "help the immune system by fighting off harmful bacteria...."

ACTUAL PRACTICE 5 - PRACTICE SET 1

Notes
Louis Pasteur made food & drink safer
→ Pasteur figured out why food spoils
→ tiny pathogens spoil food, cause disease
others believed spontaneous generation
Pasteur heated liquid at certain temp. to kill pathogens
→ called heating 'pasteurization'
→ dairy pasteurized today

Multiple-Choice Answers

1) D

   Detail Question

   According to the lecture, Pasteur's "research on how to make food and drink safer has prevented countless illnesses...."

2) B

   Inference Question

   Because an alcohol manufacturer actively sought out Pasteur's help, we can infer that *Pasteur was a well-known scientist even before he developed pasteurization*.

3) B

   Inference Question

   Because Pasteur found "tiny organisms" in the spoiled alcohol, and because the professor implies that these organisms can cause "sickness and disease," we can infer that these organisms *caused the alcohol to spoil*.

4) C

   Inference Question

   Because those who believed in spontaneous generation thought that "maggots were born from food" itself, rather than from eggs, we can infer that these people did not understand the process of *food and drink spoilage*.

5) C

   Detail Question

   For the process of pasteurization, Pasteur "determined the lowest temperature... that wine must be heated at to kill pathogens." Thus, *pasteurization occurs at a lower heat than boiling*.

6) A

   Inference Question

Because the sentence mentions how pasteurization is used today, we can infer that it was included to *connect Pasteur's discovery to the present day.*

ACTUAL PRACTICE 5 - PRACTICE SET 2

Notes

Stu. wants to start volunteer club
→ help out poor & homeless
→ ask community what its needs are
advisor says club needs uni. approval
→ gives stu. paperwork
stu. leaves to do paperwork

Multiple-Choice Answers

1) C

   Main Idea Question

   At the beginning of the lecture, the student states the reason for her visit: "I want to learn about the process of starting a campus club."

2) B

   Detail Question

   The student says that other students "want to do more to help out poor families and homeless people."

3) B

   Inference Question

   When the advisor says that the student's idea is "not very specific," he means that the *idea needs more details.*

4) D

   Detail Question

   The students wants to "recruit student volunteers" in order to "introduce volunteers to community groups." In other words, *she hopes that student volunteers can help community groups.*

5) D

   Detail Question

   At the end of the conversation, the advisor says that the student "needs to get the club approved by the university." He then *gives the student some paperwork to fill out* so she can submit her idea for a club to the university.

ACTUAL PRACTICE 5 - PRACTICE SET 3

Notes

main question: "What is a gene?"
→ gene = strip of DNA, tells body how to develop,
determines appearance, health, etc.
genes passed on from parent → offspring (sexual)
in asexual, offspring clones of parent (sea star)
in humans, 99% of genes same
→ differing genes = alleles (eye color)

Multiple-Choice Answers

1) D

   Main Idea Question

   Because the professor spends the entire lecture addressing the question, "What is a gene?" we can conclude that the main topic is *what genes are and how they create individuals.*

2) A, D

   Detail Question

   After introducing the main topic of the lecture, the professor says, "In other words, genes determine how you look, your blood type…."

3) A

   Purpose Question

   Immediately after introducing the idea that "genes get passed on from a parent to its offspring," the professor talks about sexual and asexual reproduction (*two types of reproduction*).

4) B

   Inference Question

   All the animals listed as reproducing asexually lack the complex brains and nervous systems of animals such as mammals and birds, which reproduce sexually. Thus, we can infer that *asexual reproduction tends to occur in simpler life forms.*

5) C

   Purpose Question

   The phrase "believe it or not" is a common phrase that means, "what I'm about to say may sound made-up, but it's true." Thus, we can infer that the professor says this because *a surprising fact will follow.*

6) A

   Detail Question

   According to the professor, "slightly differing genes (*variations of genes*) are called alleles."

ACTUAL PRACTICE 6 - PRACTICE SET 1

Notes

structure of atoms: protons, neutrons, electrons
→ pro./neu. = same masses, group together to form nucleus

→ elec. = less mass, travel around nucleus
electric charge: proton: +1, neutron: 0, electron: -1
prof. recaps at end

Multiple-Choice Answers

1) B

Main Idea Question

At the beginning of the lecture, the professor says, "let's start with the structure of atoms." Because he discusses atomic structure throughout the lecture, we can conclude that the main topic is *the structure of an atom*.

2) A, D

Detail Question

The professor says, "protons and neutrons…are grouped together at the center of the atom, forming the nucleus of the atom."

3) A

Purpose Question

Here, the professor begins by talking about the mass of an electron, but then he talks about another quality: electric charge. Thus, we can infer that the professor switches the topic of discussion in order *to transition to the topic of electric charge*.

4) C

Detail Question

According to the professor, "the electron has a lot less mass than the proton and neutron." Using this information, we can determine that *protons are more massive than electrons*.

5)

	Neutral charge	Positive charge	Negative charge
Proton		✓	
Neutron	✓		
Electron			✓

Inference Question

The professor says, "The electron has a negative electric charge of 1"; "the proton has a positive electric charge of 1"; and "The neutron… is electrically neutral."

ACTUAL PRACTICE 6 - PRACTICE SET 2

Notes

stu. will be traveling on day of final (June 8th)
→ *wants to take test early (June 5th)*
→ *has to take different version of test (no cheating)*

prof. trusts stu., different test = policy
stu. leaves to study for final

Multiple-Choice Answers

1) D

Main Idea Question

Early in the conversation, the professor asks the student, "so you're wondering if you can take the exam early?" The student confirms that this is true, so the student wants *to see if he can take the final exam early*.

2) C

Detail Question

The student asks the professor, "is there any way I can take the test the Friday before, so on, ah, June 5th?"

3) D

Detail Question

The professor says, "I will have to give you a different version of the test than the other students will be taking."

4) A

Purpose Question

When the student tells the professor that he "would never tell the others the questions in advance," he is saying that he does not intend to cheat on the exam. The professor's lighthearted response shows that the professor *does not think that the student cheats*.

5) B

Inference Question

At the end of the conversation, the student says, "I guess I'd better go and study for that final!"

ACTUAL PRACTICE 6 - PRACTICE SET 3

Notes

Chauvet Cave (discovered 20 yrs. ago)
→ *hidden for 25,000 yrs., has 30,000+ yr. old cave paintings*
paintings = animals, some now extinct, not used as hunting guides bec. animals shown were rarely hunted
teacher will discuss theories for paintings' purposes

Multiple-Choice Answers

1) A

Main Idea Question

In the lecture, the professor mainly discusses the "hundreds of well-preserved cave paintings" located in Chauvet Cave.

2) C

Inference Question

After the researchers moved the rocks that and entered the cave, the professor says that they "stepped thousands of years into the past," implying that the blocked cave entrance had protected the cave from invasive humans or animals. Then, the professor describes the paintings as "well-preserved." Thus, we can infer that the rocks *protected the art for 25,000 years.*

3) A

Detail Question

According to the professor, "The paintings depict more than a dozen different animal species."

4) B

Inference Question

After a student asks what purpose the drawings serve, the professor responds, "your question is one that researchers have been asking since the cave's discovery." From this, we can infer that *researchers are not sure what purpose the drawings served.*

5) A

Detail Question

The professor says that the drawings are probably not hunting guides because "Humans rarely hunted many of the animals depicted," which are mostly predator species such as *hyenas, bears, and lions.*

6) D

Inference Question

At the end of the lecture, the professor says, "Let's go over some theories about why the artists created these paintings…."

CHAPTER 4

LISTENING 1

Notes

Greek myth: Hades (Underworld, death), Persephone, Demeter (crops, harvest)
→ *Hades kidnaps Per., Demeter sad.*
→ *Demeter stops crops until Per. Returned*
→ *Hades & Demeter deal: each get ½ year w/ Per.*
myth explains seasons (summer = Per. & Demeter, winter = Per. & Hades)

Multiple-Choice Answers

1) B

Main Idea Question

The professor tells the Greek myth of Hades and Persephone, which the Greeks used to *explain why seasons occur.*

2) B

Detail Question

According to the professor, Hades "rules the kingdom that people go to after they die," so he is *associated with death.*

3) C

Purpose Question

Here, the professor is contrasting the *extremeness of Hades' actions* with actions that are considered normal, such as taking a date to dinner and a movie.

4) A

Detail Question

According to the lecture, Demeter stopped crops from growing after she "demanded that Persephone be released [from Hades], but Demeter's request was denied." Thus, Demeter *was upset that Hades took her daughter away.*

5) B

Detail Question

At the end of the lecture, the professor says, "when Persephone was with Demeter, she allowed crops to grow and flowers to bloom, explaining why plants grow so well in spring and summer."

6) D

Inference Question

Because the professor seems very familiar with the characteristics of myths, and because she says, "this is one of my favorite Greek myths," we can infer that she is *very knowledgeable about Greek mythology.*

LISTENING 2

Notes

topic: movement of stars
Earth's spinning on axis → stars appear to move
stars spin around celestial pole (N & S)
Polaris = North Star, barely seems to move = close to pole; used for navigation, Guiding Star

Multiple-Choice Answers

1) C

Main Idea Question

The professor reveals the main topic of the lecture when he says, "The apparent movements of the stars are caused by the Earth's rotation around its own axis."

2) D

Detail Question

At the beginning of the lecture, the professor says, "We've come to this location outside the city tonight to watch the motion of the stars in the sky."

3) A

Detail Question

According to the professor, "The apparent movements of the stars are caused by the Earth's rotation around its own axis."

4) A, D

Detail Question

The professor says that Polaris "is more commonly called the 'North Star,'" and that "some people call it the 'Guiding Star.'"

5)

	Celestial pole	Western horizon	Eastern horizon
Stars appear to rise here			✓
Stars appear to descend here		✓	
Stars appear to rotate around this	✓		

Inference Question

The professor says, "the Earth's rotation makes it seem like all the stars in the night sky rotate around these [celestial] poles." He also says that stars "rise on the eastern horizon and descend below the western horizon."

LISTENING 3

Notes

discussing stu. GRE score
stu. need high Eng.-lit. score for grad school
stu. has taken GRE 3 time, has taken Eng.-lit. test 2 times, score still too low
→ *Eng.-lit.* → *needs top 10% score*
→ *test on all of Eng.-lit. (very broad)*
→ *stu. reading anthologies to prepare*
→ *advisor tells stu. to research other grad. programs*
after convo. stu. will go to lib. to look up grad. schools

Multiple-Choice Answers

1) B

Detail Question

The student says, "the English-literature subject test is a real pain. I've taken it twice…"

2) A

Detail Question

The advisor asks the student about preparing for a "graduate program for English," so we can conclude that the student will study *English.*

3) C

Inference Question

The student says that his subject-test scores are "still in the mid-level percentiles." Thus, we can infer that he scored in approximately the 50th *percentile.*

4) D

Detail Question

After the advisor asks, "What will you do to prepare next time you take the test?" the student responds, "I've started reading anthologies that include the works of important English authors."

5) A

Inference Question

At the end of the conversation, the student says, "I was just going over to the library to research other programs."

LISTENING 4

Notes

early U.S. national parks (founding of Yellowstone)
1870 → *expedition explores Yellowstone region*
→ *Hedges: in expedition, promotes Yellowstone as national park*
→ *1872: Pres. Grant makes Yellowstone a national park*
→ *1890s: 4 more parks established*

Multiple-Choice Answers

1) B

Main Idea Question

At the beginning of the lecture, the professor states that the main topic is "the early history of the National Parks System." He then goes into a detailed account of the *establishment of Yellowstone*

National Park.

2) A

Detail Question

According to the professor, "a group of explorers undertook an expedition to visit" Yellowstone to investigate *strange natural wonders* such as "massive hot springs, geysers, and even a mountain of black glass."

3) A

Inference Question

Had Yellowstone been well explored before the 1800s, hunters and explorers would have already known about Yellowstone's natural wonders. Because the first reports of these natural wonders are from the 1800s, we can infer that Yellowstone *was relatively unexplored before the 1800s.*

4) B

Detail Question

According to the professor, "Cornelius Hedges... said that the Yellowstone region should be preserved as a national park."

5) C

Detail Question

The professor says, "in 1872... President Ulysses Grant established Yellowstone National Park."

6) D

Purpose Question

The phrase, "to pick up steam," means to increase in speed or momentum. Thus, the excerpt serves *to show how quickly the U.S. National Parks System developed* immediately after the founding of Yellowstone.

LISTENING 5

Notes

stu. research paper
why prof. gave stu. "C" on paper
stu. spent 1 month on paper, 10 pages long
→ paper lacks bibliography
→ stu. didn't support thesis
→ stu. repeats info. in paper (uses same quote 3 times)
→ prof. will give stu. writing tips in future
stu. = confused, mad → calmer by end of convo.

Multiple-Choice Answers

1) A

Main Idea Question

At the beginning of the conversation, the student says to the professor, "I wanted to ask you about the "C" you gave me on my research paper." Thus, she visits the professor *to ask about a grade.*

2) B

Inference Question

Because a month is a long time to spend working on a paper, we can infer that she wanted an above-average grade to reflect her hard work, not a "C." Therefore, the student probably *feels that she deserved a better grade.*

3) C

Detail Question

The first comment the professor makes to the student about her paper is "you needed to include a bibliography."

4) D

Detail Question

After telling the student that she needed a bibliography, the professor says, "there's just not enough evidence to prove your thesis here."

5) A

Detail Question

At the end of the conversation, the professor tells the student, "Drop by my office before our next paper is due and I can give you some tips." In other words, he tell the student to *talk with him before the next assignment* is due.

LISTENING 6

Notes

structure of U.S. gov. (Exec., Legis., and Jud. branches)
→ Exec: pres. in charge
→ Legis: Congress in charge, makes laws
→ Jud: Supreme Court in charge
stu.? → why 3 branches
→ colonists want to break away from Brits., who have king
→ colonists want diff. gov., no king.
→ 3 branches make sure no one too powerful, no king

Multiple-Choice Answers

1) C

Main Idea Question

At the beginning of the lecture, the professor explains the main topic by saying, "Now let's move on to the structure of the American government."

2) C, D

Detail Question

The professor explains that the three branches of government "are the Executive Branch, the Legislative Branch, and the Judicial Branch."

3) D

Detail Question

The professor says, "The head of the Executive Branch is the President of the United States…."

4) A

Purpose Question

According to the professor, "the colonists in charge of structuring the U.S. government wanted it to be different from the British monarchy." Thus, the professor mentions the British monarchy *to contrast it with the structure of the U.S. government.*

5) C

Inference Question

Because the colonists wanted a government that was different from the British monarchy, "where the kind had all the power," we can infer that the colonists *did not want one person to have all governmental power*.

6) B

Detail Question

At the end of the lecture, the professor says, "the three branches of U.S. government exist to make sure that the United States will never be ruled by a dictator, tyrant, or king." Thus, we can infer that multiple branches of government ensure that *none of them become too powerful*.

SIMPLE ANSWERS

CHAPTER 1

Main Idea Question
Practice 1
 1) C
Practice 2
 2) D
Practice 3
 3) A
Practice 4
 4) A

Detail Question
Practice 1
 1) C
 2) D
Practice 2
 3) C
 4) A, D
Practice 3
 5) B
 6) D
Practice 4
 7) A
 8) C

Purpose Question
Practice 1
 1) C
 2) A
Practice 2
 3) B
 4) D
Practice 3
 5) D
 6) A
Practice 4
 7) B
 8) C

Inference Question
Practice 1
 1) A
 2) B
Practice 2
 3) C
 4) A
Practice 3
 5) B
 6) D
Practice 4
 7) A
 8) C

Exercise 1
 1) D
 2) C
 3) B
 4) C
 5) A

Exercise 2
 1) B
 2) A
 3) B
 4) D
 5) C

Exercise 3
 1) C
 2) D
 3) A, C
 4) B
 5) D

Exercise 4
 1) B
 2) D
 3) A
 4) B
 5) A

Exercise 5
 1) C
 2) B, D
 3) A
 4) C
 5) B

CHAPTER 2

Main Idea Question
Practice 1
 1) B
Practice 2
 2) A
Practice 3
 3) C
Practice 4
 4) D

Detail Question
Practice 1
 1) D
 2) A, B
Practice 2
 3) B
 4) D
Practice 3
 5) A
 6) C, D
Practice 4
 7) B, C
 8) D

Purpose Question
Practice 1
 1) D
 2) A
Practice 2
 3) B
 4) A
Practice 3
 5) B
 6) A
Practice 4
 7) D
 8) C

Inference Question
Practice 1
 1) D
 2) A
Practice 2
 3) A, D
 4) D
Practice 3
 5) B
 6) D
Practice 4
 7) D
 8) C

Exercise 1
 1) A
 2) D
 3) C
 4) A
 5) B
 6) D

Exercise 2
 1) D
 2) A
 3) B
 4) C
 5) C
 6) A

Exercise 3
 1) D
 2) B
 3) C
 4) A
 5) A
 6) D

Exercise 4
 1) D
 2) C
 3) D
 4) A
 5) A
 6) B

Exercise 5
 1) B
 2) C
 3) A
 4) D
 5) B
 6) C

CHAPTER 3

● ACTUAL PRACTICE 1

Practice Set 1
 1) D
 2) B
 3) A
 4) D
 5) C
 6) B

Practice Set 2
1) C
2) A
3) B
4) A
5) C

Practice Set 3
1) A
2) B
3) C
4) D
5)

1)	C
2)	B
3)	D
4)	A

● ACTUAL PRACTICE 2
Practice Set 1
1) D
2) C
3) A
4) D
5) B
6) B

Practice Set 2
1) B
2) B
3) D
4) A
5) B

Practice Set 3
1) D
2) A
3) B
4) C
5) D
6) A

● ACTUAL PRACTICE 3
Practice Set 1
1) B
2) A
3) C
4) A
5) 's-Hertogenbosch - A
   Triptych - C
   The Temptation of Saint
   Anthony - B

Practice Set 2
1) B
2) A
3) D
4) D
5) B

Practice Set 3
1) A
2) B
3) C
4) B
5) C
6) A

● ACTUAL PRACTICE 4
Practice Set 1
1) C
2) A
3) C, D
4) D
5) B
6) C

Practice Set 2
1) C
2) B
3) D
4) A
5) C

Practice Set 3
1) C
2) B
3) A
4) D
5) A
6) A, C

● ACTUAL PRACTICE 5
Practice Set 1
1) D
2) B
3) B
4) C
5) C
6) A

Practice Set 2
1) C
2) B
3) B
4) D

5) D

Practice Set 3
1) D
2) A, D
3) A
4) B
5) C
6) A

● ACTUAL PRACTICE 6
Practice Set 1
1) B
2) A, D
3) A
4) C
5)

	Neutral charge	Positive charge	Negative charge
Proton		✓	
Neutron	✓		
Electron			✓

Practice Set 2
1) D
2) C
3) D
4) A
5) B

Practice Set 3
1) A
2) C
3) A
4) B
5) A
6) D

CHAPTER 4

Listening 1
1) B
2) B
3) C
4) A
5) B
6) D

Listening 2
1) C
2) D
3) A
4) A, D
5)

	Celestial pole	Western horizon	Eastern horizon
Stars appear to rise here			✓
Stars appear to descend here		✓	
Stars appear to rotate around this	✓		

Listening 3
1) B
2) A
3) C
4) D
5) A

Listening 4
1) B
2) A
3) A
4) B
5) C
6) D

Listening 5
1) A
2) B
3) C
4) D
5) A

Listening 6
1) C
2) C, D
3) D
4) A
5) C
6) B

www.ingramcontent.com/pod-product-compliance
Lightning Source LLC
Chambersburg PA
CBHW081210170426
43198CB00018B/2904